LARK JEWELRY & BEADING
beadweaving master class

RACHEL NELSON-SMITH'S

BEAD RIFFS

LARK JEWELRY & BEADING

beadweaving master class

RACHEL NELSON-SMITH'S

BEAD RIFFS

Jewelry Projects in Peyote & Right Angle Weave

LARK CRAFTS

An Imprint of Sterling Publishing Co., Inc.
New York

WWW.LARKCRAFTS.COM

Editor
Nathalie Mornu

Technical Editor
Judith Durant

Art Director
Kathleen Holmes

Junior Designer
Carol Morse Barnao

Photographer
Lynne Harty

Illustrator
Rachel Nelson-Smith

Cover Designer
Chris Bryant

Editorial Assistance
Abby Haffelt

Library of Congress Cataloging-in-Publication Data

Nelson-Smith, Rachel.
  Rachel Nelson-Smith's bead riffs : jewelry projects in peyote & right angle weave. -- 1st ed.
      p. cm.
  Includes index.
  ISBN 978-1-60059-783-1 (alk. paper)
  1. Beadwork--Patterns. 2. Jewelry making. I. Title. II. Title: Bead riffs.
  TT860.N458 2011
  745.594'2--dc22

                              2011005345

10 9 8 7 6 5 4 3 2 1

First Edition

Published by Lark Crafts
An Imprint of Sterling Publishing Co., Inc.
387 Park Avenue South, New York, NY 10016

Text and illustrations © 2011, Rachel Nelson-Smith
Photography © 2011, Lark Crafts, an Imprint of Sterling Publishing Co., Inc., unless otherwise specified
Performance photos on pages 8, 11, 18, 26, 30, and 32 © Walter Wagner

Distributed in Canada by Sterling Publishing,
c/o Canadian Manda Group, 165 Dufferin Street
Toronto, Ontario, Canada M6K 3H6

Distributed in the United Kingdom by GMC Distribution Services,
Castle Place, 166 High Street, Lewes, East Sussex, England BN7 1XU

Distributed in Australia by Capricorn Link (Australia) Pty Ltd.,
P.O. Box 704, Windsor, NSW 2756 Australia

The written instructions, photographs, designs, patterns, and projects in this volume are intended for the personal use of the reader and may be reproduced for that purpose only. Any other use, especially commercial use, is forbidden under law without written permission of the copyright holder.

Every effort has been made to ensure that all the information in this book is accurate. However, due to differing conditions, tools, and individual skills, the publisher cannot be responsible for any injuries, losses, and other damages that may result from the use of the information in this book.

If you have questions or comments about this book, please contact:
Lark Crafts, 67 Broadway, Asheville, NC 28801
828-253-0467

Manufactured in China

ISBN 13: 978-1-60059-783-1

For information about custom editions, special sales, and premium and corporate purchases, please contact the Sterling Special Sales Department at 800-805-5489 or specialsales@sterlingpub.com.

For information about desk and examination copies available to college and university professors, submit requests to academic@larkbooks.com. Our complete policy can be found at www.larkcrafts.com.

DEDICATION

This book is dedicated to the memory of Mitchell Wayne Pruiett. He believed I could do great things and would have loved to see me do this.

CONTENTS

INTRODUCTION

**BEADING IS LIKE JAZZ. THERE'S A MULTITUDE OF
APPROACHES TO TAKE WITH IT.**

In beadwork, we begin by getting used to the needles. We figure out which thread to use, and we learn how to read a pattern. Musicians learn to play an instrument, whereas beaders learn stitches.

More experienced beaders begin to experiment with combinations of beads and stitches. In jazz, skilled artists go beyond the notes and chords written on the sheet music and allow their personal experience and surroundings to affect the notes. Improvisation gives way to infinite exploration.

I've spent 10 years singing jazz and almost two decades beading. I approach beading in the way a jazz musician approaches playing: I make it up as I go, from moment to moment. This book offers you instructions for 23 of my beaded jewelry designs. Every project contains unexpected combinations and reflects my willingness to thread off the beaten path and attempt the untried.

You won't have to wing it, though. The book starts with a section called The Setup that describes all the materials and tools you'll need. This chapter also explains all the stitches step by step, with helpful illustrations.

Then it's on to the projects, most of which begin with a base of right angle weave and progress into variations of tubular peyote stitch. (This has a direct parallel in jazz—you first play the chords and the melody and then progress into impromptu creating.) Many of the pieces feature bling-blingy chaton montées and sparkly rivoli crystals. When you wear them, you'll shine like a star. The projects include glamorous necklaces and pendants, baubles for your ears and fingers, and bangles to grace your wrists.

My instructions walk you through the steps for making the pictured jewelry. But if you want to make the project more your own, sidebars called Riff It suggest ways to do just that, empowering you just like a music master class.

Because I so love jazz, I named each project after a facet of it. You might see a musician's name: Sassy (page 86) was the nickname of velvety crooner Sarah Vaughan, for example. It could be a concept in jazz music theory, such as Swing Time (page 97). I've even named projects after some of my favorite tunes, including "Four" and "Billie's Bounce" (pages 94 and 38).

In jazz, if one note is off, you play the third note a little off and everything begins to fit. Same thing goes for beading. Take a listen to Ella Fitzgerald's 1960 live recording of "Mack the Knife" on *Ella in Berlin,* in which she forgets the lyrics and completely changes them. The album was ultimately inducted into the Grammy Hall of Fame in 1999. Talk about turning a slip-up into something wonderful!

That's exactly why I improvised as I designed these projects for you—I knew we'd end up with marvelous jewelry and great beading fun.

Rachel Nelson-Smith

CHAPTER ONE
THE SETUP

As it is with jazz, so it is with beadwork. While there's much room for improvisation and playful experimentation, it must first start with a foundation. In jazz, the foundation consists of chords, tune form, and melody. With beadweaving, the base encompasses materials, tools, and techniques. The goal of both is the same—a lasting result, something that endures. Like "All Blues" by Miles Davis, Dizzy Gillespie's "Night in Tunisia," or Ella Fitzgerald's version of "A-Tisket, A-Tasket," in beadweaving the objective is to make works of beauty that stand the test of time.

This section describes the materials, tools, and techniques I use. Although a wide world of materials is available, I use these selected items to make jewelry of enduring beauty.

The projects found between the covers of this book are mainly composed of two simple materials—beads and thread.

Materials

The objects of our attention are made of glass and crystal.

Seed Beads

I use glass seed beads from Japan, where manufacturers have brought a high level of skill to their production. Japanese seed beads are exceptional for their wide range of gorgeous colors and comparatively large holes. I mix beads from various manufacturers in the same way I mix stitches.

Crystals

In my work, if it's not a Japanese seed bead, then it's a crystal. A number of manufacturers produce these, but Swarovski crystals shine through the projects in these pages. (I choose that brand for the crystals' singular brilliance, but you can go with any manufacturer.) I use bicones, rounds, and two styles of montées—rose montées and chaton montées. A rose montée is short and has four prongs to hold a stone. A chaton montée also has prongs to hold the stone but its setting is taller. I use rivolis, too; they're flashy crystal cabochons. Mostly crystal AB stones have been used here to keep things simple yet sparkling.

Benny (on the sax) and I listen to Kent do a solo on the piano, as Drew plays the changes on his bass and keeps time with the drummer, Steve.

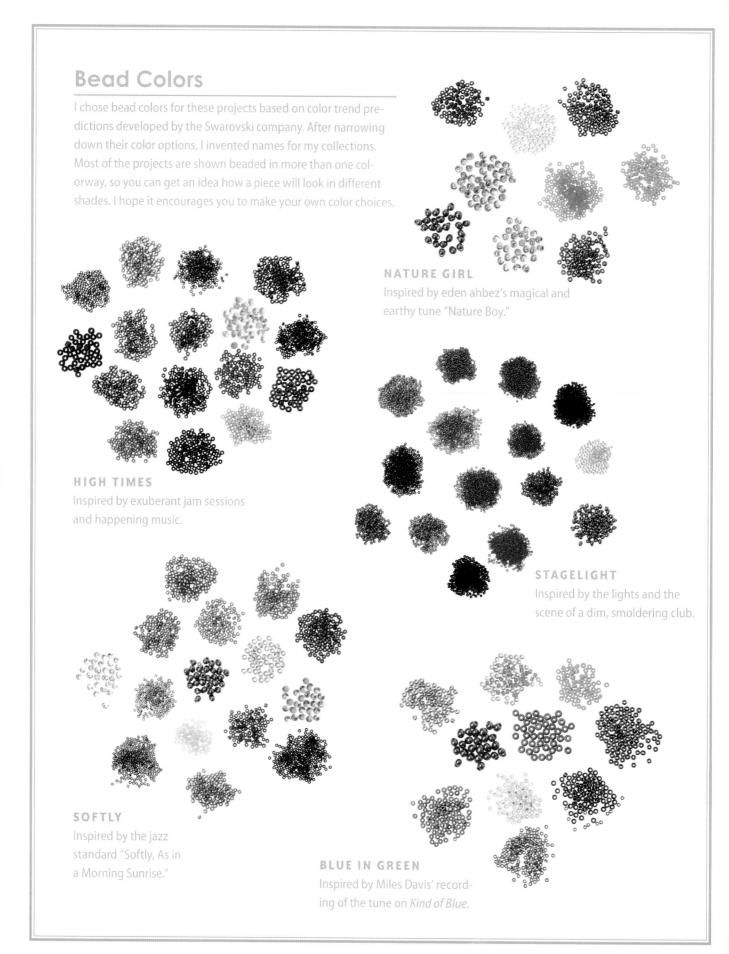

Bead Colors

I chose bead colors for these projects based on color trend predictions developed by the Swarovski company. After narrowing down their color options, I invented names for my collections. Most of the projects are shown beaded in more than one colorway, so you can get an idea how a piece will look in different shades. I hope it encourages you to make your own color choices.

NATURE GIRL
Inspired by eden ahbez's magical and earthy tune "Nature Boy."

HIGH TIMES
Inspired by exuberant jam sessions and happening music.

STAGELIGHT
Inspired by the lights and the scene of a dim, smoldering club.

SOFTLY
Inspired by the jazz standard "Softly, As in a Morning Sunrise."

BLUE IN GREEN
Inspired by Miles Davis' recording of the tune on *Kind of Blue*.

Thread

I choose thread for each of my projects based on color, size, strength, workability, and stability. Is the color appropriate for the beads—will it blend, or will it be used as a design feature? Is it thin or thick enough—how many times will I pass through the bead with the smallest hole? Will the thread produce a stiff or a supple result? How long will it last in each separately functioning section of a piece? Compare the requirements of a particular project with the attributes of various threads to determine your final choice.

Most of the beadwork in this book was assembled with KO thread, selected for color and size. I also use the medium gray Silamide A, since that shade isn't in the KO color palette. I choose Fireline 6 lb. test for extra strength when working with metal beads.

Thread Treatment

The projects presented here were worked without any thread treatment except what the thread manufacturers added. If you need more tension when working a piece, run the thread through beeswax.

Working Length of Thread

Some people use long lengths of thread to avoid having to stop to end old and begin new lengths. Others use short lengths to prevent knots and avoid repetitive arm extensions. I go short. To measure out a length, I hold the thread bobbin at my body center with one hand, and with the thread in the other I extend my arm and repeat, pulling out about 60 inches (152 cm).

Findings

Findings are used to hold jewelry together and to attach it around the body. They come in a plethora of forms and materials, and perform a multitude of functions. I incorporate jump rings, lobster-claw clasps, lengths of chain, and several styles of ear wires chosen to complement and finish projects. I also use liquid silver, slim silver beads in the shape of tiny tubes. These are traditionally associated with Native American jewelry.

Tools

A few basic tools are needed to make any piece of beadwork. It's simple: the essential tools for beadweaving are scissors and needles. Scissors, or snips as I like to call them, should have small, sharp blades and tips for close, clean cuts of thread ends. I use size 12 beading needles almost exclusively; I don't recommend sharps because of their comparatively large diameter. And use a light-hued velvet or lambskin suede for a comfortable work surface that prevents beads from rolling away.

Beadweaving Kit

Size 12 beading needles

Thread in a variety of colors

Sharp snips

Suede or velvet work surface

Beyond the Usual Tools

For a customized experience, round up the following.

- A needle case (beaded, of course)

- A lighter to melt away threads too short to snip

- A task lamp with a full-spectrum bulb

- A comfortable chair for extended beading sessions

- A tin or other container for discarded items like excess thread, needle envelopes, and abandoned beadwork

- A triangular bead scoop for cleanup

- A mini funnel for returning beads to tubes

- A small dish for misshapen and stray beads

- Two pairs of chain-nose pliers, to work with jump rings and to force the needle through tight spaces

- Flush wire cutters to remove extra loops on multistrand clasps

Non-essential tools that make beading easier include (clockwise from top left) a lighter, a mini funnel, a bead scoop, and a beaded needle case.

Techniques

When I first started beadweaving, I gathered irregular beads, dental floss, wire cutters, and a sewing needle, then made rudimentary strips of square-stitched beadwork. Thousands of beading hours later, I've learned a great deal. I share that with you here.

Double Knot

Most projects in this book begin with a number of beads tied into a ring with a simple double knot. String the beads and, leaving a 6-inch (15.2 cm) tail, overlap the tail and working thread to tie a simple overhand knot. Tie a second knot and leave the tail to weave in later.

Terminology and Convention

A bandleader swings his finger through the air or nods his head to communicate with his group. My modus operandi will be to explain to you with words and illustrations.

- When there's a series of rows or steps in a single illustration, the steps are color-coded in this order: red, blue, green, black, gold, purple, and pink.

- The beads being added are outlined in fuchsia and beads already added are outlined in black.

- I'm right-handed, which guides the orientation of the illustrations.

Nearly two decades after I made them, my first pieces are still held together by my novice stitches. They prove that dental floss is a strong beading material!

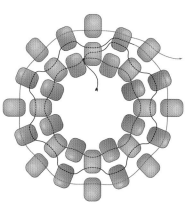

figure 1

Peyote Stitch

A beadweaving technique widely known from ancient to modern times, peyote stitch is extremely simple and useful. In its basic form, peyote stitch is like a swing tune at 140 beats per minute—it sounds pretty good and is easy to listen to. When we go beyond the basics, it's like saxophonist Charlie Parker shredding on his tune "Yardbird Suite" at 220 beats per minute. You'll usually work with a single thread, but a doubled thread is used when a project or section needs extra strength, or when larger beads, such as 8° round seed beads, are used.

A key aspect of peyote is the initial beads strung always become rounds 1 and 2 when round 3 is added. The peyote basics presented here are 1-drop stitches, adding one bead at a time, but they may be applied to other drop variations with smooth and textural—as well as increased and decreased—results.

• A smooth surface results from adding the same number of beads in each opening as the number of beads two rounds below.

• A textural or changing surface results from adding a different number of beads in an opening as the number of beads two rounds below. For example, you might add one bead rather than two in the fourth round for a decrease.

For these projects I use the tubular even-count and flat odd-count variations. Flat even-count is the basic form of the stitch and though it's not used for these projects, I recommend an exploration if you haven't yet encountered it. Flat odd-count peyote stitch is used just once, in Polka Dots and Moonbeams (page 34), so it's described there.

Tubular Even-Count Peyote Stitch

The projects in this book use only the even-count version of the stitch, which means that the same number of stitches is added in each round and there's a "step up" at the end of every round to get into position for the next round.

Thread a needle with a working length of thread. Rounds 1 through 4 are shown in figure 1. ***Note:*** The 4-bead 1-drop version with only two beads in each round is used many times in the projects. The current row must always be reinforced before the step up, or the tube won't hold shape.

Rounds 1 and 2 String an even number of beads—16-bead 1-drop is shown in this example. Tie a simple double knot to form a circle and pass through the first bead added (red line).

Round 3 String one bead, skip a bead, and pass through the next bead; repeat to the end of the round. Pass through the first bead added in this round again—this is the step up (blue line).

Round 4 String one bead and pass through the next bead added in the previous round; repeat to the end of the round. Step up through the first bead added in this round.

Repeat round 4 to desired length.

Thread Ends

Hide the beginnings and ends of threads within the beads for the appearance of effortless mastery. This applies to all forms of peyote stitch.

To end a thread, select three beads on a diagonal from the last bead exited. Pass under the thread between the last bead exited and the first bead in the diagonal, then pass under the loop formed by the thread exiting the bead. Pass through the first bead in the diagonal and pull up the slack to pull the tightening knot inside the bead. Repeat through the second and third beads on the diagonal, then cut the thread close to the third bead (figure 2).

To begin a new thread, weave to the area where the beadwork is to continue. Leaving a short tail, work the series of knots as above, then cut the thread close to the first bead.

Right Angle Weave

Once learned, right angle weave presents limitless possibilities for structure and texture. When working a strip of right angle weave, it *seems* possible to follow a number of thread paths, which can cause confusion. However, there's only one correct thread path. If you follow the rules described below and on the next page, it will become intuitive, much like basic arithmetic, where two plus two always equals four, and like jazz, where with experience, improvisation and syncopation become instinctual.

Rule 1 Each subsequent unit travels in a circular direction opposite from the previous unit. For example, a unit formed with a clockwise thread path is followed by a unit formed with a counterclockwise thread path.

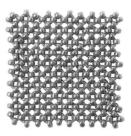

1-Drop

1/3-Drop

3/3/3/4- and 1/3/2/3-Drops in 11° and 15°

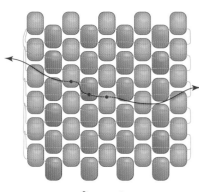

figure 2

Rule 2 Each subsequent stitch travels at roughly a right angle from the previous stitch. For example, each horizontal stitch is followed by a vertical stitch.

Rule 3 Each unit has four sides and four angles—usually 90° each. Even when the four angles of a unit don't each measure 90°, they always add up to 360°.

Always begin with four beads or four sets of beads. Stitch everything twice for stability. This means you need to duplicate the last unit before going on to the next unit, provided there's ample hole space for any necessary additional stitches.

Several variations of right angle weave with varying bead counts are possible, such as 1-drop with one bead on all four sides; a combo of 1/3-drop with one bead on two sides and three beads on two sides; or 3/3/3/4- and 1/3/2/3-drops where several sides are different, such as in 'Round Midnight (page 65). The stitch pattern follows the same sequence of turns no matter how many beads are on each side.

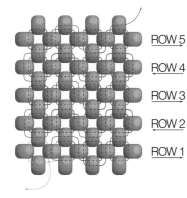

figure 3

Flat Even-Count Right Angle Weave

This example, shown in figure 3, is simple 1-drop, and row 1 is worked from left to right. Note that all units with a red line are worked clockwise and all units with a blue line are worked counterclockwise.

Row 1, Unit 1 String four beads and tie a simple double knot to form a square. Working counterclockwise, pass through the first bead added (gray line).

Row 1, Unit 2 String three beads and, working clockwise, pass through the last bead exited and the first two beads just added (red line).

Row 1, Unit 3 String three beads and, working counterclockwise, pass through the last bead exited and the first two beads just added (blue line).

Remaining Unit(s) in Row 1 and Turnaround Continue alternately repeating units 2 and 3. To add the final unit, work as for unit 2 but end by passing through only the first bead just added (red line).

Row 2, Unit 1 String three beads and, working counterclockwise, pass through the last bead exited, the first, second, and third beads just added, and the next bead in the previous row (blue line).

Row 2, Unit 2 String two beads and, working clockwise, pass through the third bead of the previous unit, the bead in the previous row, and the first bead just added (red line).

Row 2, Unit 3 String two beads and, working counterclockwise, pass through the next bead of the previous row, the first bead of the previous unit, the two beads just added, and the next bead in the previous row (blue line).

Remaining Unit(s) in Row 2 and Turnaround Continue alternately repeating units 2 and 3. To add the final unit, work as for unit 2 but end by passing through the first and second beads just added (red line).

Row 3, Unit 1 String three beads and, working counterclockwise, pass through the last bead exited, and the first bead just added (blue line).

Row 3, Unit 2 String two beads and, working clockwise, pass through the bead in the previous row, the first bead of the previous unit, the two beads just added, and the next bead in the previous row (red line).

Row 3, Unit 3 String two beads and, working counterclockwise, pass through the second bead of the previous unit, the bead in the previous row, and the first bead just added (blue line).

Remaining Unit(s) in Row 3 and Turnaround Continue alternately repeating units 2 and 3. To add the final unit, work as for unit 2 but end by passing through only the first bead just added.

Repeat from row 2, unit 1 through row 3 and turnaround to desired length.

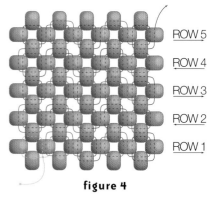

Flat Odd-Count Right Angle Weave

This is worked like even-count right angle weave except that each row will have an odd number of units. To begin, work row 1 as for even-count, repeating units 2 and 3, then repeating unit 2 once more. The rows are outlined in figure 4.

Row 1 Turnaround To add the final unit, work as for unit 3 but end by passing through all three beads just added (blue line).

Row 2, Unit 1 String three beads and, working clockwise, pass through the last bead exited and the first bead just added (red line).

Row 2, Unit 2 String two beads and, working counterclockwise, pass through the next bead in the previous row, the third bead in the previous unit, the two beads just added, and the next bead in the previous row (blue line).

ROW 5
ROW 4
ROW 3
ROW 2
ROW 1

figure 4

There's nothing like singing a scat solo.

Row 2, Unit 3 String two beads and, working clockwise, pass through the second bead added in the previous unit, the bead in the previous row, and the first bead just added (red line).

Remaining Units in Row 2 and Turnaround Continue alternately repeating units 2 and 3, then unit 2 once more. To add the final unit, repeat unit 3 but end by passing through the first and second beads just added.

Row 3, Unit 1 String three beads and, working counterclockwise, pass through the last bead exited and the first bead just added (blue line).

Row 3, Unit 2 String two beads and, working clockwise, pass through the next bead in the previous row, the first bead added in the previous unit, the two beads just added, and the next bead in the previous row (red line).

Row 3, Unit 3 String two beads and, working counterclockwise, stitch through the second bead added in the previous unit, the bead in the previous row, and the first bead just added (blue line).

Remaining Units in Row 3 and Turnaround Continue alternately repeating units 2 and 3, then unit 2 once more. To add the final unit, repeat unit 3 but end by passing through the first and second beads just added.

Repeat from row 2, unit 1 through row 3 and turnaround to desired length, adding thread as needed.

At left, many rows are joined to form a large tube or bezel. On the right, three rows become a tube.

Tubular Right Angle Weave

You can join the edges of any rectangular strip of flat right angle weave to form a tube. Following the principles of the stitch, join the two ends of the strip together, adding one bead at a time (figure 5).

Thread Ends

To end a thread and hide the securing points, select a series of three beads on a diagonal from the last bead exited. Pass under the thread between the bead last exited and the first bead in the diagonal, then pass under the loop formed by the thread exiting the bead. Pass through the first bead in the diagonal and pull up the slack to tighten the knot inside the bead. Repeat through the second and third beads on the diagonal, then cut the thread close to the third bead (figure 6). To begin a new thread, weave to the area where the beadwork is and continue working in right angle weave, cutting the tail end when the connections are secured.

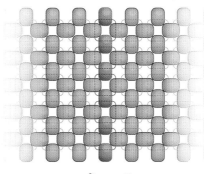

figure 5

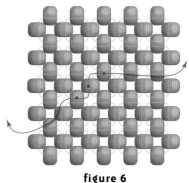

figure 6

Bumps

Like a soloist improvising over chord changes, we add dimension to right angle weave bases with a variety of bumps. Bumps are worked in tubular peyote stitch up from right angle weave units. The first rounds of peyote are usually worked with beads of the same size used in the base, and some continue with a smaller size bead for a smooth finish. The exception comes when a diagonal shape is created with three sizes of beads, as for Night in Tunisia (shown on the previous page).

Round 1 of each bump is a transition from right angle weave to tubular even-count peyote. The final round of each bump is a cinch round—you'll pass through the last round of beads in a circular pattern and pull the thread taut. The exceptions are the 1-drop bump and 9-drop riser, which are not cinched. Bumps can be finished with montées or finial beads.

Once you've completed a bump, weave through the beadwork to begin the next bump. **Note:** Some of the thread paths in the illustrations may appear loose, with a considerable amount of thread exposed. This is for illustration purposes only—you should add each round of beads in the bumps with a fair amount of tension.

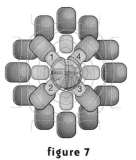

figure 7

Finish with Montées Choose two opposing beads in the final round and pass through these beads and the montée as follows. With the thread exiting clockwise from bead 1, string one montée, pass through bead 2 clockwise, pass through the montée, pass through bead 3 clockwise, pass through the montée, pass through bead 4 clockwise, and pass through the montée. Repeat from the beginning for a total of eight passes through the montée (figure 7).

Finish with Finial Beads A 2-mm round silver bead atop a bump adds a nice finishing touch. Pass through a bead in the final round. String a 2-mm bead and pass through the bead in the final round directly opposite the first one exited. Moving in a counterclockwise direction, pass through the next bead in the final round, through the 2-mm bead, and through the bead in the final round directly opposite the last bead exited (figure 8). Repeat the entire thread path twice.

figure 8

1-Drop Bump

This drop is worked from a 1-drop right angle weave base—or a cinch—into 1-drop tubular peyote stitch; it's possibly the trickiest of all the bumps to make. Use the same size bead for the bump that you used for the base. Reinforce each round before beginning the next round. All steps are shown in figure 9.

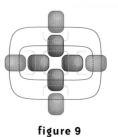

figure 9

Round 1 Weave through the beadwork to exit from any bead in the 1-drop right angle weave unit. String one bead and pass through the opposite bead of the same unit. String one bead and pass through the first bead exited. Step up by passing through the first bead added (shown with a red line).

Round 2 and Subsequent Rounds String one bead and pass through the next bead from the previous round. String one bead and pass through the next bead from the previous round, then step up through the first bead added (blue line). Repeat round 2 to desired length.

20

2-Drop Bump

Decreasing the bead size in round 3 brings this bump in for a smooth, rounded finish. Beads are indicated by A and B, and you can use combinations of 11°s and 15°s; 8°s and 11°s; or 6°s and 8°s, with the larger bead (the A) being the same size as the right angle weave base beads. This is a four-round bump pattern; to make a taller bump, repeat round 2. All rounds are illustrated in figure 10.

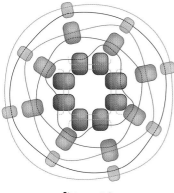

figure 10

Round 1 Weave through the base to exit from the second base bead on any side of a 2-drop unit. String one A and pass through the second base bead of the next side of the same unit. Repeat three more times. Step up at the end of the round by passing through the first A added (shown with a red line).

Round 2 String one A and pass through the next A of the previous round. Repeat three more times (blue line). Step up through the first A added.

Round 3 String one B and pass through the next A of the previous round. Repeat three more times (green line). Step up through the first B added.

Round 4 String one B and pass through the next B of the previous round. Repeat three more times (black line). Step up through the first B added.

Cinch Pass two times through the last four Bs added to form a circle (gold line) and pull up taut.

3-Drop Bump

This bump begins on a 3-drop right angle weave base and becomes a 1-drop tubular peyote stitch. A decrease in bead size in round 2 brings this bump in for a smooth, rounded finish, but you may use only one size of bead for five rows, as in Night Star (page 41). Beads are indicated by A and B, and you can use combinations of 11°s and 15°s; 8°s and 11°s; or 6°s and 8°s, with the larger bead (the A) being the same size as the right angle weave base beads. ***Note:*** To make a taller bump, repeat round 2 several times with A, then change to B in round 3. All steps are shown in figure 11.

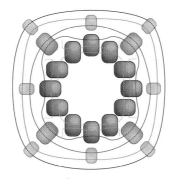

figure 11

Round 1 Weave through the base to exit the second base bead on any side of a 3-drop unit. String one A and pass through the second base bead on the next side of the same unit. Repeat three more times. Step up at the end of the round by passing through the first A added (shown with a red line).

Round 2 String one B and pass through the next A in round 1. Repeat three more times. Step up through the first bead added (blue line).

Round 3 String one B and pass through the next B in round 2. Repeat three more times. Step up through the first bead added (green line).

Cinch Pass two times through the last four Bs added to form a circle (black line) and pull up taut.

Flat 3-Drop Bump

This is a flat version of the 3-drop bump, also worked on a base of 3-drop right angle weave. Simply work round 1 and cinch, skipping rounds 2 and 3 (figure 12).

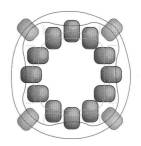

figure 12

22

Round 3 String one 15° and pass through the next 15° in round 2. Repeat three more times. Step up through the first bead added (green line).

Cinch Pass two times through the last four 15°s to form a circle (black line) and pull up taut.

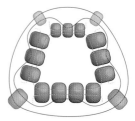

Flat 3/3/3/4-Drop Bump

This bump is worked up from the same base as 3/3/3/4-drop bump with only one row of tubular peyote. Round 1 and the cinch are shown in figure 14.

3/3/3/4-Drop Bump

In the spirit of variations on a theme, this bump incorporates two sizes of beads—11°s and 15°s—and is worked on a right angle weave base of the same two sizes. It begins with 11°s and finishes with 15°s. Additional rounds of 11°s or 15°s may be added to increase the height. See figure 13 for all rounds.

Round 1 Weave through the beadwork to exit the second 15° in the set of three. String one 15° and stitch through the middle 11° on the next side of the unit. String one 11° and stitch through the middle two 11°s on the next side of the unit. String one 11° and pass through the middle 11° on the next side of the unit. String one 15° and stitch through the middle 15° on the next side. Step up through the first 15° added (red line).

Round 2 String one 15° and pass through the next 15° or 11° in round 1. Repeat three more times. Step up through the first bead added (blue line).

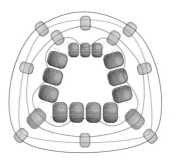

figure 13

figure 14

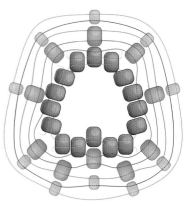

figure 15

3/4/5/4-Drop Bump

This bump is worked on a modified right angle weave base of 11°s. It begins with 11°s and finishes with 15°s. See figure 15 for all rounds.

Round 1 Weave through the beadwork to exit the third base bead of the 4-drop left side of the unit in a clockwise direction. String one 11° and pass through the second base bead of the next (3-drop) side. String one 11° and pass through the second and third base beads of the next (4-drop) side. String one 11° and pass through the second base bead of the next (5-drop) side, then string one 11° and pass through the fourth base bead of the same (5-drop) side. String one 11° and pass through the second and third base beads of the next (4-drop) side. Step up at the end of the round by passing through the first bead added (figure 15, red line).

Round 2 String one 11° and pass through the next 11° in round 1. Repeat four more times. Step up through the first bead added (blue line).

Row 3 String one 15° and pass through the next 11° in round 2. Repeat four more times. Step up through the first bead added (green line).

Row 4 String one 15° and pass through the next 15° in round 3. Repeat four more times. Step up through the first bead added (black line).

Cinch Pass two times through the last five 15°s to form a circle (gold line) and pull up taut.

4-Drop Bump

This bump begins on a 4-drop right angle weave base and then alternates between 1- and 2-drop even-count peyote stitch. Use the same size bead for the bump as was used for the base. The 4-drop bump in Rondo (page 44) and in Groove (page 74) remains 1-drop for all three rows. **Note:** To make a taller bump, repeat rounds 2 and 3 alternately, then finish with round 4 and the cinch. All steps are shown in figure 16.

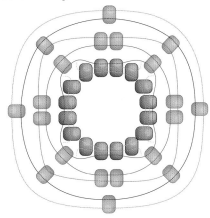

figure 16

Round 1 Weave through the base to exit the third bead on any side of the 4-drop unit. String one bead and pass through the second and third base beads on the next side of the unit. Repeat three more times. Step up at the end of the round by passing through the first bead added (shown with a red line).

Round 2 String two beads and pass through the next bead in round 1. Repeat three more times. Step up through the first two beads added (blue line).

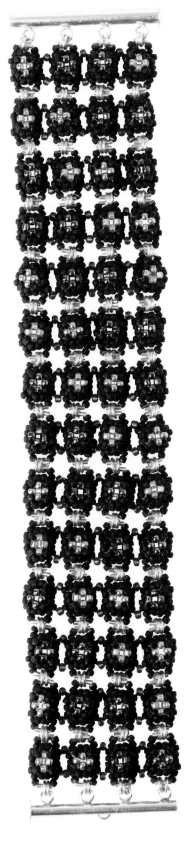

Row 3 String one bead and pass through the next two beads in round 2. Repeat three more times. Step up through the first bead added (green line).

Row 4 Pick up one bead and pass through the next bead in round 3. Repeat three more times. Step up through the first bead added (black line).

Cinch Pass two times through the last four beads to form a circle (gold line) and pull up taut.

4-Drop Diagonal Bump

This one's worked on a 4-drop right angle weave base of 11°s. It begins with 8°s and 11°s and finishes with 15°s. Follow along with figure 17.

Round 1 Weave through the base to exit the third bead on the left side of a unit in a clockwise direction. String one 8° and pass through the second and third base beads on the next side of the unit. String one 11° and pass through the second and third base beads on the next side of the unit. Repeat to add one more 8° and one more 11°. Step up by passing through the first 8° added (shown with a red line).

Round 2 String one 15° and pass through the next 11° in round 1. String one 15° and pass through the next 8° in round 1. Repeat to add two more 15°s (blue line).

Cinch Pass two times through the 8°s and the 15°s to form a circle (green line) and pull up taut.

5-Drop Bump

This bump starts on a 5-drop right angle weave base of 11°s and works into a 1-drop even-count peyote stitch. You'll begin with 11°s and finish with 15°s. For a taller bump, repeat round 2, then go on to rounds 3 through the cinch. Refer to figure 18 as you work.

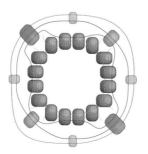

figure 17

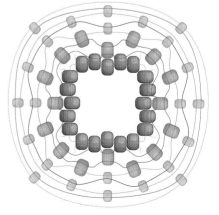

figure 18

Round 1 Weave through the base to exit the second bead on any side of a 5-drop unit. *String one 11° and pass through the fourth bead on the same side of the unit. String one 11° and pass through the second bead on the next side of the unit. Repeat from * three more times. Step up by passing through the first 11° added in the round (shown using a red line).

Round 2 String one 11° and pass through the next 11° in round 1. Repeat seven more times. Step up through the first 11° added in the round (blue line).

Round 3 String one 15° and pass through the next 11° in round 2. Repeat seven more times. Step up through the first 15° added in the round (green line).

Round 4 String one 15° and pass through the next 15° in round 3. Repeat seven more times. Step up through the first 15° added in the round (black line).

Round 5 String one 15° and pass through the next two 15°s in round 4. Repeat three more times. Step up through the first 15° added in the round (gold line).

Round 6 String one 15° and pass through the next 15° in round 5. Repeat three more times. Step up through the first 15° added in the round (purple line).

Cinch Pass two times through the last four 15°s twice to form a circle (pink line) and pull up taut.

9-Drop Riser

Worked up from a 9-drop right angle weave base, a riser is similar to a bump but left open. In Something Cool (page 108), the 9-drop riser has a bezeled rivoli stitched into the opening. It's worked in the same size bead that was used for the base. All steps are shown in figure 19.

Round 1 Weave through the base to exit the eighth bead on any side of the unit. String one bead and pass through the second bead on the next side of the unit. String one bead and pass through the fourth bead on the same side. String one bead and pass through the sixth bead on the same side. String one bead and pass through the eighth bead on the same side. Repeat three more times. Step up by passing through the first bead added in the round (this is shown with a red line).

Round 2 and Subsequent Rounds String one bead and pass through the next bead in the previous round. Repeat 15 more times. Step up through the first bead added in the round (blue line). Repeat round 2 to the desired height.

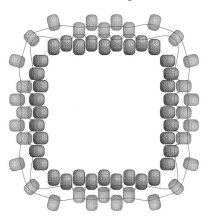

figure 19

Right Angle Weave Bezel

Flat right angle weave is stitched into a tube and cinched on both openings to close up and form a bezel around a stone. The front and back bezel openings can be cinched with the fast method, the slow method, the super-fast method, or a combination of any two methods. There are nine possible combinations; each is directly related to the size and shape of the stone. Often, the first time you encounter a particular stone, it may take several attempts to get the fit correct. It's a balance between making the bezel wide enough to hug the edges and stay in place while revealing the maximum amount of the stone's face. Figure in the combinations of units in width and length and there are limitless variations in bezeling a single stone. The unit counts for bezels for 12- and 18-mm rivolis and 27-mm stones are included with each set of project instructions, as is the cinch style you should use. Close the first side with the stone set aside. Close the second side with the stone held in place.

Base Work a strip of 1-drop right angle weave two or more rows wide. The width depends on the depth of your stone, and the length depends on the circumference.

Close the Tube Bring the short ends of the strip together and stitch in one final unit to join as in Tubular Right Angle Weave (page 19).

Slow Cinch Weave through the tube to exit an up bead on the edge of either opening. String one bead—the same size as the base beads—and pass through the next up bead. Repeat all the way around the opening, tightening slightly as you go (figure 20). If more tightening is needed, repeat the thread path.

Fast Cinch Weave through the tube to exit an up bead on the edge of either opening. String one bead—the same size as the base beads—and pass through the next two up beads. Repeat all the way around the opening, tightening slightly as you go (figure 21). Be careful not to use too much tension. If more tightening is required, repeat the thread path.

Super-Fast Cinch Weave through the tube to exit an up bead on the edge of either opening. Pass through the next up bead without adding a bead. Repeat all the way around the opening, tightening slightly as you go (figure 22). Be careful not to use too much tension. If you need to tighten more, repeat the thread path.

Finishing Touches and Findings

A live performance flows from beginning to end, but the final moments are the most memorable, no matter what came before. After all, the end is when a grand finale takes place. I see each of these projects as a performance, with the finishing touches and findings as the final moments of that performance.

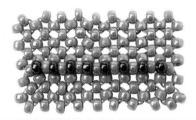

The dark beads are ditch beads.

Ditch Beads

With this method, you stitch beads into the small gaps between units of right angle weave. I use it to embellish, to merge right angle weave into flat peyote stitch, and to add layers. You can work on a flat piece or on a tube section. Weave through the beadwork to exit any bead in the row you want to add beads to.

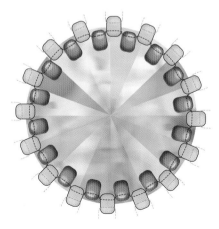

figure 20

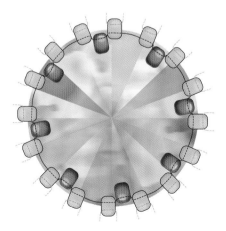

figure 21

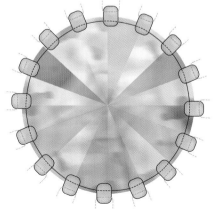

figure 22

String one bead and pass through the next base bead with a hole oriented in the same direction. Repeat as needed. Weave through the end unit to turn around and embellish the next base row in the same manner if desired (figure 23).

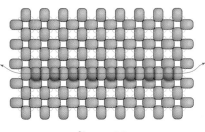

figure 23

Right Angle Weave
Base Embellishment

Endless entertainment and possibilities crop up when pairing simple embellishment with this versatile stitch. You may stitch a bead to units containing any number of beads, and many sizes of embellishment beads will work. The stitch is shown here on the diagonal (figure 24). Simply stitch a bead over the openings of right angle weave units. With the thread exiting counterclockwise through the top of a unit, pass through the embellishment bead—here, a bicone is shown—clockwise through the bottom and left side of the unit, through the embellishment bead again, then counterclockwise through the right side of the unit. Repeat the thread path to secure.

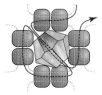

figure 24

Embellishing with Montées

Rose and chaton montées add an elegant finishing touch when stitched to flat and tubular variations of right angle weave and peyote stitch.

Montée to 1-Drop Right Angle Weave
This is worked in the same way as for finishing bumps with montées. See figure 7.

Montée to 2-Drop Right Angle Weave
With the thread exiting clockwise from bead pair 1, string one montée, pass through bead pair 2 clockwise, pass through the montée, pass through bead pair 3 clockwise, pass through the montée, pass through bead pair 4 clockwise, and pass through the montée (figure 25). Repeat from the beginning for a total of eight passes through the montée.

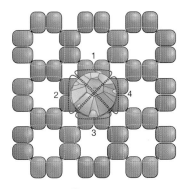

figure 25

Montée to 1-Drop Flat Peyote Stitch
With the thread exiting one of the beads to be embellished, pass through the montée, pass through the next bead in the same direction as the previous pass, and pass through the montée (figure 26). Repeat from the beginning for a total of eight passes through the montée.

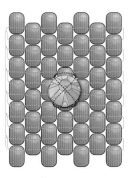

figure 26

Montée to 1-Drop Tubular Peyote Stitch Tube End With the thread exiting from a bead in the final row, pass through the montée, pass through the other bead in the final row in the same direction, and pass through the montée (figure 27). Repeat for a total of eight passes through the montée.

Beaded Toggle Closure

I use plastic rings, sold in the notions section of fabric and craft stores, that have an outer diameter of ¾ to 1½ inches (1.9 to 3.8 cm). To make the toggle loop, cover the ring with 1-drop tubular right angle weave and stitch in a closed jump ring or liquid silver as follows. The number of units will vary by ring and bead size and by the amount of tension you use while stitching.

Round 1 Work a strip of 1-drop right angle weave that's one unit short of the circumference of the ring's band. With the thread exiting a bead of the last unit, string one bead and pass through a bead from the first unit, then string one bead and pass through a bead of the last unit (figure 28). Close as in Tubular Right Angle Weave (page 19).

figure 27

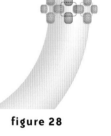

figure 28

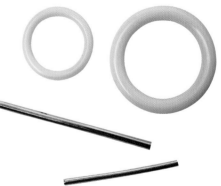

Plastic rings and heavy wire make perfectly matching halves of a toggle closure when covered in beading.

Round 2 and Subsequent Rounds Work a row of 1-drop right angle weave from the previous row (figure 29, red line). Add one bead to close the round (blue line). Repeat until the tube is one unit short of the length of the ring's band.

figure 29

Close the Tube Exit one end bead of the last unit, string one bead, and pass through the corresponding bead of the first unit. String one bead and pass through the bead in the final unit again. Repeat to close the tube around the band (figure 30).

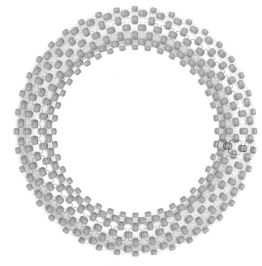

figure 30

Add Closed Jump Ring With the thread exiting from any bead in the unit, pass through the closed jump ring, the opposite bead in the unit, the closed jump ring, and the first bead again (figure 31). Repeat to secure.

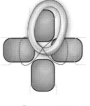

figure 31

If desired, embellish the outer units with 3.5-mm montées. Stitch the first montée two units away from the closed jump ring. If the number of units is even, stitch the montées in every other unit. If the number is odd, skip two units between each montée except the first and last.

To make the toggle bar, flush cut a length of heavy wire (18- to 12-gauge) equal to twice the inside diameter of the finished toggle loop. Cover the length of wire with tubular 1-drop right angle weave. At the midpoint, stitch in a closed jump ring, liquid silver, or attach directly to a chain link. Add a series of double jump ring connections until the bar is centered. Add montées to the ends, if desired.

Drew swings while I sing.

Liquid Silver

Liquid silver is another name for metal bugle beads. Several sizes are available; I prefer those about 4–5 mm long. I use them to protect thread from wear at connection points, but they can be applied to any beadwoven surface, too.

Add to Surface of 1-Drop Right Angle Weave
This method is used with 15°s in Dolled Up (page 112), and it would work with 11°s as well. Weave through the beadwork to exit any base bead in a unit. String one seed bead, one liquid silver, and one seed bead; pass through the opposite base bead in the unit, the seed bead last strung, the liquid silver, and the first seed bead added; repeat the thread path until no space remains within the bead holes. It may also be used to attach liquid silver to the surface of 1-Drop Peyote Stitch (figure 32).

figure 32

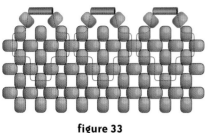

figure 33

Add to Edge of 1-Drop Right Angle Weave

This method is used with 11°s in Swing Time (page 97), and it would work with 15°s as well. If you're adding multiple liquid silver beads to align with the loops of a multistrand clasp, be sure to space the connections correctly. Weave through the beadwork to exit any up bead in the final edge row. String one seed bead, one liquid silver bead, and one seed bead; skip one up bead and pass through the next up bead. To secure the liquid silver just added, repeat the thread path shown in figure 33 until no space remains within the bead holes. Weave through the beadwork and repeat to add more liquid silver beads as needed.

Jump Rings

In all their simplicity, jump rings are some of the most useful findings. Use both open and closed jump rings to attach findings to finished beadwork.

Closed Jump Rings Closed, also known as soldered, jump rings consist of a length of wire formed into a circle; the ends of the wire are soldered together to completely close the circle. They're put to use in the projects presented here as connection points between beadwork and clasp attachments, and they work great with 1-drop right angle weave, a final cinch row, and 1-drop tubular peyote.

Join with 1-Drop Right Angle Weave or a Final Cinch Row Select two beads on opposite sides of the same right angle weave unit. Exit the first bead, string the closed jump ring, pass through the second bead in the same direction as the first, and pass back through the jump ring. Repeat the thread path until the connection is secure. Generally, the number of securing stitches depends on the thread thickness and hole size. When I'm asked how many stitches to make, I answer, "Do it until you're bored or the hole fills up." Use the same method as for adding jump rings to a toggle closure (this was described in figure 31).

Join with 1-Drop Tubular Peyote Select two beads two rows apart with one direction on top of the other. Add a jump ring as in 1-drop right angle weave or final cinch row (see above).

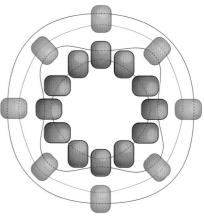

figure 35

Open Jump Rings Open jump rings consist of a length of wire formed into a circle, but the ends are not joined together. To open a jump ring, hold a pair of chain-nose pliers in each hand, or a pair of chain-nose pliers in one hand and a pair of flat-nose pliers in the other. Grasp the jump ring close to the opening with the pliers in your nondominant hand. These pliers should simply hold the jump ring steady for the rest of the operation. Next, grasp the jump ring on the other side of the opening with the pliers in your dominant hand and swing the ring open (figure 34). Slip the opened jump ring through the pieces to be connected and swing it closed with the pliers in your dominant hand.

figure 34

Double Jump Ring Connections I use these for extra strength with more weighty projects and on the bar end of a toggle clasp. Simply use two rings where you'd normally use one.

Bead Caps

Bead caps add a nice detail to your beadwork. I typically make 3-Drop Bead Caps using size 11° seed beads, working with a single thread and repeating the thread path in each round.

Refer to figure 35 for all steps. String 12 beads, form a circle, and tie a simple double knot leaving a 6-inch (15.2 cm) tail. Pass through the first bead strung (red line).

Round 1 String one bead, skip two beads, and pass through the next bead. Repeat three times. Step up by passing through the first bead added in the round (blue line).

Round 2 String one bead and pass through the next bead added in round 1. Repeat three more times (green line).

Cinch Pass through the four beads added in round 2 and repeat the thread path. Pull up taut (black line).

Crimp Beads and Flexible Beading Wire

Crimping is a neat and secure way to attach clasps to beading wire. Cut a length of flexible beading wire 4 inches (10.2 cm) longer than the finished piece. String the beads and components as desired on the wire. String the first end of the wire through a crimp bead, through the loop of the first clasp finding, and back through the crimp bead. Close the crimp bead with chain-nose or crimping pliers. Tuck the excess wire—1 inch (2.5 cm) or less—inside the end beads. Repeat with the second end of the wire, tucking the excess length of wire into the end beads before crimping.

CHAPTER TWO

NECKLACES
AND PENDANTS

Made in High Times colorway

POLKA DOTS
AND MOONBEAMS

The lyrics to "Polka Dots and Moonbeams" are delightful and a little corny, referring to a "pug-nosed dream." The melodic content moves in steps, ascending and descending—much like the design of this necklace.

▶ Overview

Right angle weave tubes become beads for stringing, and you'll work flat pieces of peyote stitch beadwork off of ditch beads on some of the tubes, decreasing the edges to points. Then you'll add montées for embellishment, string the components onto flexible beading wire, and finish with a beaded toggle or purchased clasp.

▶ Tubes

With a single thread and 11°s, work a rectangle of 1-drop right angle weave that is five units long and three units wide (figure 1, red line). Close to form a tube by adding a total of six 11°s one at a time (blue line). Reinforce all units as they are added. Make 21 tubes—14 will be strung as they are and 7 will become components.

▶ Components

With double thread and 11°s, add four ditch beads to a lengthwise row of a tube (figure 2). Turn around to add four beads in the second row, add the fifth bead by stitching under the thread added in the

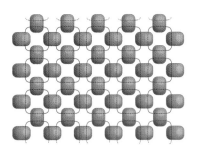

figure 1

figure 2

SUPPLIES

Size 11° red iris metallic round seed beads, 15 g

Size 8° red iris metallic round seed beads, 7 pieces

7 crystal AB chaton montées, 5 mm

16 crystal AB rose montées, 3.5 mm

38 crystal AB bicones, 4 mm

16 crystal AB bicones, 3 mm

23 inches (58.4 cm) of flexible beading wire, medium weight

Supplies for beaded toggle, or a purchased clasp

2 crimp tubes, 2 x 2 mm

Size 12 beading needles

Red thread

Sharp snips

Suede or velvet work surface

TECHNIQUES

Tubular Right Angle Weave

Ditch Beads

Montée to 1-Drop Flat Peyote Stitch

Beaded Toggle Closure (optional)

Crimp Beads with Flexible Beading Wire

FINISHED SIZE

Chain, 20 inches (50.8 cm) long

Central component, ½ x 2 inches (1.3 x 5.1 cm)

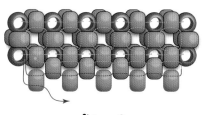

figure 3

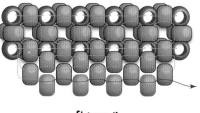

figure 4

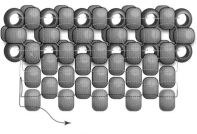

figure 5

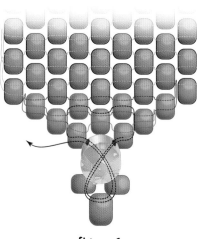

figure 6

right angle weave base, and pass back through the bead (figure 3). Add four beads in the third row (figure 4). Turn around, adding four beads in the fourth row, add the fifth bead by stitching under the thread added in the second row turn-around, and pass back through the bead (figure 5). Work 30 more rows of odd-count flat peyote stitch off the ditch beads, then decrease the beadwork to a point as follows, referring to figure 6.

Row 1 Add three 11°s as usual. Pick up the final 11°, pass under the thread before the last bead of the previous row, and pass back through the bead just added (red line).

Row 2 String one 11° and pass through the next 11° of the previous row. Repeat two more times. Turn around by catching the thread and passing back through the bead just passed through and the last bead added (blue line).

Row 3 String one 11° and pass through the next 11° of the previous row. Repeat once more. Turn around by catching the thread and passing back through the bead just passed through and the last bead added (green line).

Row 4 String one 5-mm chaton montée, one 11°, one 8°, and one 11°; pass through the chaton and the next 11° of the previous row. Repeat the thread path to secure (black line).

Repeat all steps to make six more components as follows.

Components 2 and 3 Work 22 rows of peyote stitch, then work rows 1 through 4.

Components 4 and 5 Work 14 rows of peyote stitch, then work rows 1 through 4.

Components 6 and 7 Work six rows of peyote stitch, then work rows 1 through 4.

▶ Embellish with Montées

Attach montées to the peyote stitch surface with a single thread as follows.

Component 1 Stitch one 3.5-mm rose montée to rows 4 and 6, one to rows 12 and 14, one to rows 20 and 22, and one to rows 28 and 30.

Components 2 and 3 Stitch one 3.5-mm rose montée to rows 4 and 6, one to rows 12 and 14, and one to rows 20 and 22.

Components 4 and 5 Stitch one 3.5-mm rose montée to rows 4 and 6 and one to rows 12 and 14.

Components 6 and 7 Stitch one 3.5-mm rose montée to rows 4 and 6.

▶ Finish

Referring to the photo on page 34, assemble the necklace on beading wire in this order: component 1, one 4-mm crystal, component 2, one 4-mm crystal, component 4, one 4-mm crystal, component 6, one 4-mm crystal, one 3-mm crystal, and one 4-mm crystal. *String one tube, one 4-mm crystal, one 3-mm crystal, and one 4-mm crystal; repeat from * six more times. Beginning on the other side of component 1, repeat the pattern using components 3, 5, and 7. Make a toggle closure if desired. Attach the toggle or clasp ends to the beading wire with the crimp beads.

RIFF IT

• Don't vary the lengths of the components; instead, make the necklace from nothing but short components.

This variation, beaded up in the Nature Girl colorway, uses more components, fewer tubes, and 3.5- and 5-mm rose montées with only a single 8° for embellishment at the bottom of the components.

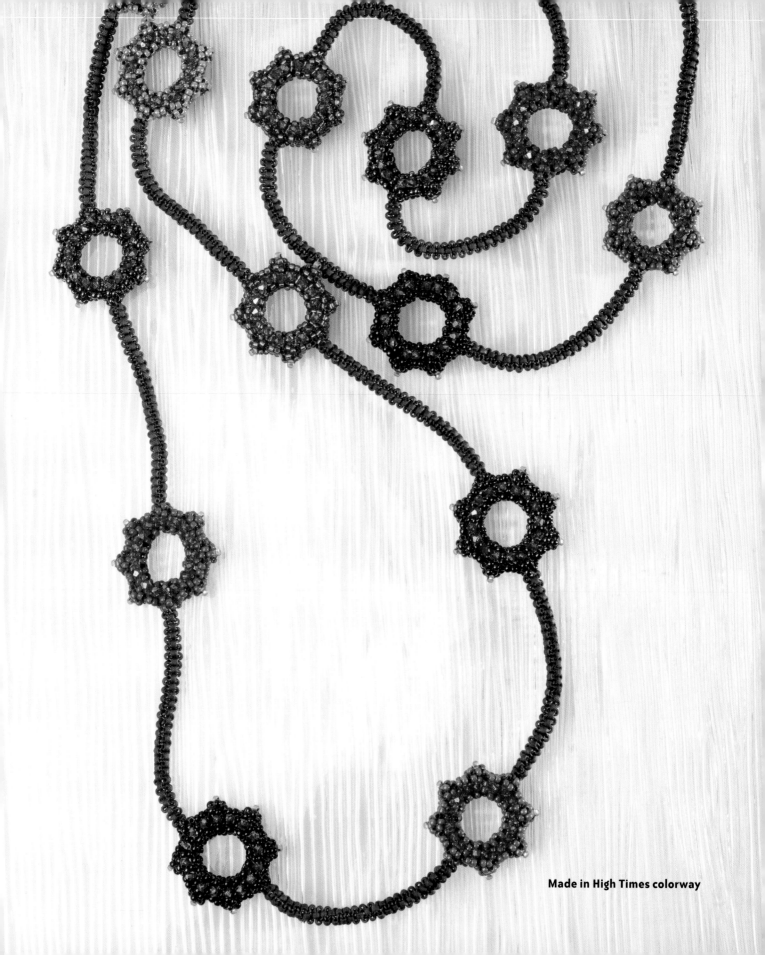

Made in High Times colorway

BILLIE'S BOUNCE

Lengths of peyote stitch connect components together—the beaded rings bob and they wiggle, evoking the melody line of Charlie Parker's tune "Billie's Bounce." Throw in lyrics by Eddie Jefferson for a riotously good time.

▶ Overview

A series of right angle weave and peyote wheels are embellished with two different techniques, then connected together with tubular peyote stitch.

▶ Wheel Base

Following the instructions below, make two right angle weave wheels each in colors A, B, C, D, E, F, G, and H, for a total of 16 wheels. Steps 1 through 4 are shown in figure 1. Work with a single thread and reinforce each base for strength and stiffness.

1 To make the first unit, string seven beads, tie a simple double knot, leaving a 6-inch (15.2 cm) tail to be worked in later, and pass through the first two beads again.

2 For subsequent units, *string five beads and pass through the last two beads exited and the first four just added. String five beads and pass through the last two beads exited and the first three just added. Repeat from * six times. String two beads, pass through the two end beads of the first unit, string one bead, and pass through the two end beads of the last unit added and the two beads just added (red line).

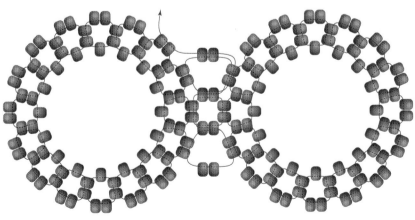

figure 1

SUPPLIES

Size 11° round seed beads:

   A, burnt sienna opaque, 4 g

   B, olive metallic, 4 g

   C, lavender opaque AB, 4 g

   D, blue metallic iris, 4 g

   E, maroon metallic iris, 4 g

   F, olive opaque, 4 g

   G, dark blue metallic, 4 g

   H, olive silver-lined, 4 g

   I, light topaz matte silver-lined, 1 g

   J, charcoal matte metallic, 12 g

512 topaz bicone crystals, 4 mm

Size 12 beading needles

Red thread

Sharp snips

Suede or velvet work surface

TECHNIQUES

Right Angle Weave

1-Drop Bump

2-Drop Bump

Finish with Finial Beads

Right Angle Weave
Base Embellishment

FINISHED SIZE

58 inches (1.5 m) long

3 Repeat steps 1 and 2 to make a second base in the same color.

4 Weave through beads to exit any set of two beads on the outside edge of the first base. String two beads and pass through a set of two beads on the edge of the second base. String two beads, pass through the last two beads exited of the first base, the first two beads added, and the two beads of the next unit of the second base (blue line). Continue to connect the bases with two beads at a time.

5 Weave through the beads to exit a bead on the inside edge of the first base. String one bead and pass through a bead on the edge of the second base. String one bead and pass through the last bead exited on the first base, the first bead added, and the next bead of the second base. Continue to connect the bases with one bead at a time (figure 2).

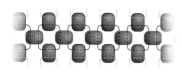

figure 2

▶ Wheel Embellishment

1 Weave through the beadwork to any 2-drop opening on the wheel edge. Embellish the opening of the base edge with one round of the 2-drop bump pattern in the same color as the base. Cinch the round and add a finial bead of color I. Repeat to add a 2-drop bump to every other opening, and make the seventh and fifteenth bumps without finial beads.

2 Weave through the beadwork to exit any set of two beads on the outer edge of the face on one side of the wheel. Add a 4-mm crystal to all 16 openings. Repeat on the other side of the wheel.

Repeat steps 1 and 2 to embellish all 16 wheels.

▶ Finish

Working with a wheel in color A, weave through the beadwork to exit any of the four beads in the cinch of a 2-drop bump where a finial bead was not added. Work the bump into 50 rows of a 1-drop bump, adding two Js in each row, one at a time. Stitch the final row to a finial-free bump on the next wheel, color B. Repeat to attach all wheels in this order: A, B, C, D, E, F, G, H, D, A, B, C, H, E, F, G—or improvise your own arrangement.

NIGHT STAR

Slipping into her gig dress for the millionth time—it's worth it. With this sparkler suspended over her heart, this singer's ready for another long night at the lounge, with the band backing her up.

Made in Stagelight colorway

SUPPLIES

Size 11° round seed beads:

  A, opaque black, 2 g

  B, hematite matte, 1 g

5 crystal AB rose montées, 3.5 mm

6 crystal AB bicones, 3 mm

Size 15° hematite matte round seed beads, 1 g

1 crystal AB rivoli, 18 mm

Silver chain necklace 18 inches (45.7 cm) long

Size 12 beading needles

Black thread

Sharp snips

Suede or velvet work surface

TECHNIQUES

Right Angle Weave

3-Drop Bump

Montées

Right Angle Weave Base Embellishment

FINISHED SIZE

1½ inches (3.8 cm) in diameter

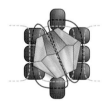

The back of the pendant

▶ Overview

A base of right angle weave closed into a tube and embellished with 3-drop bumps, montées, and crystals encircles the rivoli. You'll decrease the front and back openings to snugly enclose the stone, then string a necklace chain through a six-bead loop at the top of the pendant.

▶ Base

With a single thread and As, string eight beads and tie an overhand knot to form a ring. Pass through the first three beads strung. *String nine beads; pass through the last three beads exited and the first six beads just strung. String five beads; pass through the last three beads exited and the first four beads just strung. Repeat from * four more times until you have six small and five large loops (figure 1, red line). String three beads, pass through the three side beads of the first unit, pick up three beads, and pass through the first three beads of the last unit to close the row into a tube (blue line).

▶ Embellishment

*Add a 3-drop bump to a large right angle weave unit using Bs for round 1 and As for rounds 2 through 5. Cinch row 5 and add one montée. Weave back down to the base and add one crystal bicone between the bump and the next large unit as shown in figure 2. Repeat from * five more times but do not add a montée to the sixth bump.

figure 1

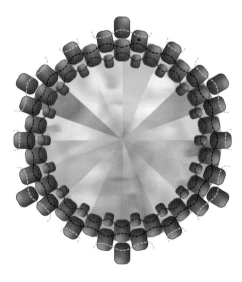

figure 2

figure 3

▶ Rivoli Bezel

Using As and 15°s, work from the front and back edges of the right angle weave base to add two rows of tubular peyote stitch as follows.

Front Side

Refer to figure 3 for rounds 1 and 2. Work loosely and reinforce each round before moving to the next step.

Round 1 Working clockwise with the thread exiting a set of three As (shown with a red dot), * string one A and pass through the next A sticking out. String one A and pass through the first A in the next set of three As from the edge of the base. String one A and pass through the third A in the same set of three As. Repeat from * five more times. Step up through the first A added in the round (red line).

Round 2 String one 15° and pass through the next A added in the previous round. Repeat 15 more times (blue line).

Back Side

Work round 1 as for the front side. Place the rivoli face forward in the bezel, then work round 2 as for the front to encase the stone.

Color variations in High Times (left) and Blue in Green

▶ Finish

With the thread exiting one of the front-most As in the cinch round of the unembellished bump, string six 15°s, pass through the corresponding back-most A, back through the front-most A, and through the six 15°s (figure 4, red line). Secure the six 15°s to the other front and back As. Repeat two more times to reinforce. String the necklace chain through the six-bead loop.

figure 4

RIFF IT

• Hang the pendant from a stitched-in closed jump ring instead of a bead loop.

• Make enough components for a bracelet—you'll probably need five or six of them. As you bead, stitch closed jump rings to the final rows of opposing bumps of the components and link them together sequentially with double jump rings.

• Make two components and attach each to an ear wire.

Made in Blue in Green colorway

RONDO

A rondo is an upbeat song with a beginning thematic passage that's repeated after every other section. Likewise, this project is an upbeat neckpiece with a thematic pattern repeated every other section. A tribute to Dave Brubeck's legendary tune "Rondo à la Turk" in 12/8 and 9/8 time, it works up a little magic with 12-bead bumps over a 16-bead base, 4-bead bumps over an 8-bead base, and 8-bead bumps over a 12-bead base.

▶ Overview

You'll bead a tubular right angle weave base around a vinyl tube core, stitch bumps onto the large units, and embellish each 1-drop unit with a rose montée. The tube ends are closed with decreasing peyote stitch, and closed jump rings are attached for connecting to the clasp. Make your own beaded toggle or purchase one and attach it with jump rings.

▶ Base

Working in right angle weave with a single thread, weave the base around the vinyl tubing as follows. Use the side beads of the first unit to complete the last unit in each round, closing the beadwork around the tube, then weave through the beadwork to get into position to begin the next round. Begin with round 1 at the bottom of figure 1 on page 46.

Round 1 Work alternating units of eight As and two As/one B/two As/one B.

Round 2 Work alternating units of one B/two As/one B/two As and four Bs.

Round 3 Repeat round 1.

Round 4 Work alternating units of one B/three As/one B/two As and four Bs.

Round 5 Work alternating units of 12 As and three As/one B/three As/one B.

SUPPLIES

Size 11° round seed beads:

    A, olive metallic, 22 g

    B, peach-lined aqua, 9 g

    C, silver-lined turquoise AB, 8 g

    D, opaque green, 6 g

    E, yellow silver-lined matte AB, 2 g

204 round sterling silver beads, 2 mm

200 crystal AB rose montées, 3.5 mm

18 inches (45.7 cm) of ¼-inch (6.4 mm) vinyl tubing

2 closed silver 20-gauge jump rings, 4 mm

12 open silver 20-gauge jump rings, 4 mm

Supplies for beaded toggle, or a purchased clasp

Size 12 beading needles

Green thread

Sharp snips

Suede or velvet work surface

TECHNIQUES

Right Angle Weave

2-Drop Bump

3-Drop Bump

4-Drop Bump

Finish with Finial Beads

Montées to 1-Drop Right Angle Weave

Tubular Peyote Stitch

Jump Rings

Beaded Toggle Closure (optional)

FINISHED SIZE

17⅝ inches (44.8 cm) long

Round 3
Round 2
Round 1
Round 2
Round 3
Round 4
Round 5
Round 6
Round 7
Round 6
Round 5
Round 4
Round 3
Round 2
Round 1

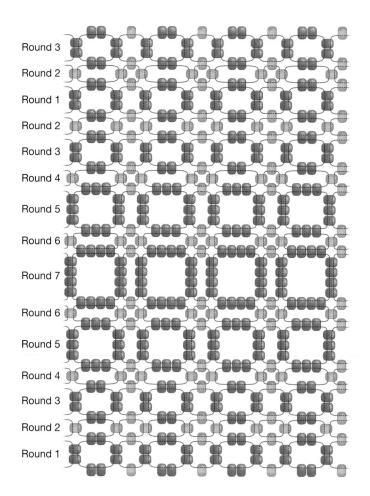

figure 1

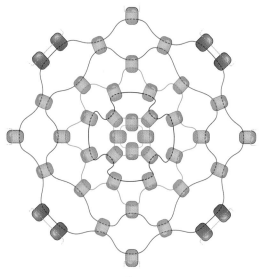

figure 2

Round 6 Work alternating units of one B/four As/one B/three As and four Bs.

Round 7 Work alternating units of 16 As and four As/one B/ four As/one B.

Subsequent Rounds Work round 6 to round 1 and then back up to round 7. Repeat the sequence, finishing with any round with alternating edge beads of two As and one B to match the outer bead pattern of figure 2—rounds 1, 2, or 3.

▶ Embellish

Working around the diameter of the tube, embellish the multi-drop units with bumps topped with finial beads (2-mm rounds) and add rose montées along the way, reinforcing all thread paths. **Note:** Though the rounds are given below in numerical order, begin with any round, work up to round 7, then back down to round 1. Repeat working rounds 1 through 7 and then rounds 6 through 1, ending the last repeat with rounds 1, 2, or 3.

Round 1 With As, embellish each 2-drop unit with one round of a 2-drop bump, cinch, then add a finial bead.

Round 2 Embellish each 1-drop unit with one rose montée.

Round 3 With Cs, embellish each 2-drop unit with one round of a 2-drop bump, cinch, then add a finial bead.

Round 4 Repeat round 2.

Round 5 Embellish each 3-drop unit with two rounds of a 3-drop bump using Ds for round 1, and Cs for round 2. Cinch, then add a finial bead.

Round 6 Repeat round 2.

Round 7 Embellish each 4-drop unit with only three rounds of a 4-drop bump using Es for round 1, Ds for round 2, and Cs for round 3. Cinch, then add a finial bead.

▶ Finish the Ends

Cut the vinyl tube at the final round. Work the final right angle weave base round into tubular peyote stitch with B as follows. Refer to figure 2 for all rounds.

Round 1 With the thread exiting two As in the final round of the base, string one B and pass through the next B of the same base round; string one B and pass through the next two As of the same base round. Repeat three more times. Step up through the first bead added (red line).

Round 2 String one B and pass through the next B of the previous round. Repeat seven more times. Step up through the first bead added (blue line).

Round 3 Repeat round 2 (green line).

Round 4 String one B and pass through the next two Bs of the previous round. Repeat three more times. Step up through the first bead added (black line).

Round 5 String one B and pass through the next B in round 4. Repeat three more times. Step up through the first bead added (gold line).

Cinch Pass through the four beads added in round 5 twice and pull taut (pink line).

Stitch a closed jump ring to the round 5 beads. Repeat at the other end of the necklace.

▶ Finish

Bead a toggle closure if desired. Attach it, or a purchased clasp, to the closed rings at the ends of the necklace with six jump rings on each side—two jump rings at each connection.

Color variations in Stagelight (above) and High Times

Made in Nature Girl colorway

PHRASEOLOGY

As the band plays the turnaround, the sax player pauses for a deep breath, then dives headlong into a bevy of notes strung together in cognitive, musical thought. He breathes in again and repeats the riff as though it's written in stone rather than the transient smolder of the night. In the same way those short phrases organize into a longer expression, in this necklace stitches come together in a statement of bead phraseology.

▶ Overview

The piece begins with a base of 11°s woven over a vinyl tube core. It's then embellished with bumps, 15°s, 8°s, and drops, and finished with a custom bead and loop closure. **Note:** Often in tubular stitches the term "step up" is used. Here we use "step down," coordinating with the figures.

▶ Base

With a single thread, weave a base over the tube core with size 11° round seed beads as follows.

Round 1 Begin 3-drop netting by stringing three Es and one A five times; tie a simple double knot, leaving a 6-inch (15.2 cm) tail to weave in later. Pass through the first two Es again to step down (figure 1).

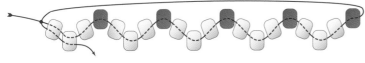

figure 1

SUPPLIES

Size 11° round seed beads:

A, matte brown AB, 10 g

B, bronze metallic, 20 g

C, olive brown silver-lined, 20 g

D, matte opaque eggshell, 15 g

E, matte aqua, 10 g

F, transparent turquoise, 10 g

G, matte dark brown, 10 g

Size 15° round seed beads:

H, bronze metallic, 2 g

I, white ceylon silver-lined, 2 g

Size 8° round seed beads:

J, matte green iris metallic, 4 g

Size 3.4-mm drop beads:

K, mint-lined transparent topaz, 85 pieces

L, matte opaque eggshell, 45 pieces

M, dark topaz silver-lined, 40 pieces

N, matte light topaz AB, 40 pieces

¼-inch (6 mm) vinyl tubing, 24 inches (61 cm) long

Size 12 beading needles

Gray thread

Sharp snips

Suede or velvet work surface

TECHNIQUES

Right Angle Weave

Ditch Beads

3-Drop Bump

4-Drop Bump

1-Drop Bump

FINISHED SIZE

20¾ inches (52.7 cm) long

figure 2

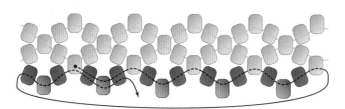

figure 3

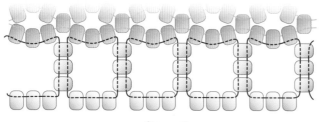

figure 4

figure 5

Round 2 String three Fs and pass through the middle E from the previous round (the second of the set of three beads). Repeat four more times. Step down through the first two Fs added in this round (figure 2).

Round 3 String one A, one F, and one A; pass through one F from the previous round (the second bead of the next set of three beads). Repeat four more times. Step down through the first A, the first F, and the second A added in this round (figure 3).

Round 4 With Es, work 3-drop right angle weave by passing through one A, one F, and one A in round 3, as shown in figure 4. Step down through the first E in a set of three. **Note:** These units will be filled in later with 3-drop bumps.

Round 5 With B, change to 3-drop netting as shown in figure 5. Step down through the first two beads added in this round.

Round 6 Work another round of 3-drop netting with Gs (figure 6). Step down through the first two beads added in this round.

Round 7 Repeat round 6 with B.

Round 8 Repeat round 6 with G.

Round 9 Repeat round 6 with B, but at the end of the round, step down through only the first B added in this round.

Round 10 Change from netting to herringbone stitch: String two 11°s of any color, then pass through the third bead of the current set of three in the previous round. Pass through the first bead in the next set of three in the previous round. Repeat four more times with different color beads in sets of two (two D, B, C, D, and F are shown in figure 7). Step down through the first bead added in this round.

Round 11 To continue in modified herringbone stitch, *string two beads (of the same color as the last bead exited) and pass through the second bead in the set of two in the previous round. String one 15° I and pass through the first bead of the next set of two beads in the previous round. Repeat from * four times (figure 8). Step down through the first bead added in the previous round and through the first bead added in this round.

Rounds 12–14 Repeat round 11.

Round 15 String one 11° E and pass through the next bead of the two-bead set, then string one 15° I and pass through the first bead of the next two-bead set. Repeat four times (figure 9). Step down through the first bead added in this round.

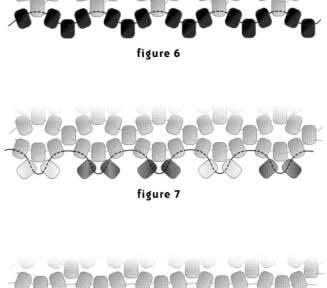

figure 6

figure 7

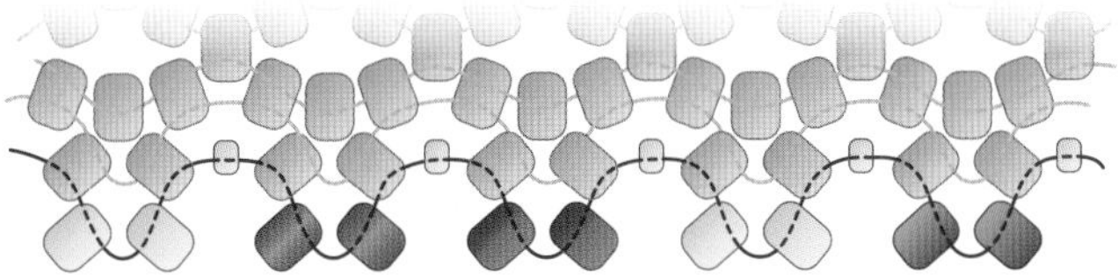

figure 8

figure 9

figure 10

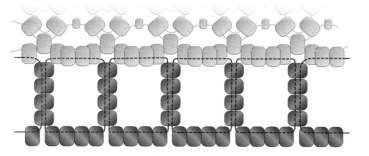

figure 11

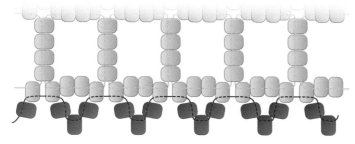

figure 12

figure 13

Round 16 String four Bs and pass through the next E in round 15. Repeat four times (figure 10). Step down through the first four beads added in this round.

Round 17 With B, create a round of 4-drop right angle weave as shown in figure 11. Step down to exit the first bead in any set of four on the beadwork edge. ***Note:*** These units will be filled in later with 4-drop bumps.

Round 18 To work 3-drop netting, string three As and pass through the fourth B of the current set of four and the first B of the next set of four (figure 12). Repeat four times. Step down through the first two beads added in this round.

Round 19 Work a round of 3-drop netting with Es (figure 13). Step down through the first two beads added in this round.

Round 20 Repeat round 19 with Fs.

Round 21 Repeat round 19 with Cs.

Round 22 Repeat round 19 with Bs.

Round 23 Repeat round 19 with As.

Round 24 Repeat round 19 with Es.

Round 25 Repeat round 19 with Fs.

Repeat rounds 3 through 25 seven more times, then repeat rounds 3 through 9, or end with any round of 3-drop netting.

▶ **Embellishment**

Following the instructions below and referring to figure 14 (working top to bottom), add embellishment in the ditches of 3-drop netting and add 3-drop and 4-drop bumps to the right angle weave spaces. (The fuchsia bead outline distinguishes the beads being added from the beads in the base, and a red dot indicates a pass through a base bead.) The round numbers below indicate the round of the base to which beads are being added. You'll also add 3-drop and 4-drop bumps to the right angle weave spaces. Work with doubled thread or secure all beads with a second pass of single thread.

Round 1 With the thread exiting the middle bead of a set of three 11° Es, add one 15° H, one 8° J, and one 15° H; pass through the middle bead of a set of three Es. Repeat four more times.

Round 2 With the thread exiting the middle bead of a set of three 11° Fs, add one 15° I, one drop K, and one 15° I; pass through the middle bead of a set of three Fs. Repeat four more times.

Round 4 Add 3-drop bumps with 11°s to the right angle weave spaces. Work rounds 1 and 2 with four Cs, and round 3/cinch with four Ds.

Round 7 With the thread exiting the middle bead of a set of three 11° Bs, add one 15° H, one drop L, and one 15° H; pass through the middle bead of a set of three Bs. Repeat four more times.

Round 8 With the thread exiting the middle bead of a set of three 11° Gs, add one 15° H, one 8° J, and one 15° H; pass through the middle bead of a set of three Gs. Repeat four more times.

Round 17 Add 4-drop bumps with 11°s. Work round 1 with four Bs, round 2 with eight Bs, round 3 with four Fs, and round 4/cinch with four Es.

Round 18 With the thread exiting the middle bead of a set of three 11° As, add one 15° H, one drop M, and one 15° H; pass through the middle bead of a set of three As. Repeat four more times.

Round 19 With the thread exiting the middle bead of a set of three 11° Es, add one 15° H, one drop N, and one 15° H; pass through the middle bead of a set of three Es. Repeat four more times.

Round 20 With the thread exiting the middle bead of a set of three 11° Fs, add one 15° I, one drop K, and one 15° I; pass through the middle bead of a set of three Fs. Repeat four more times.

Repeat the embellishments for the entire length of the base.

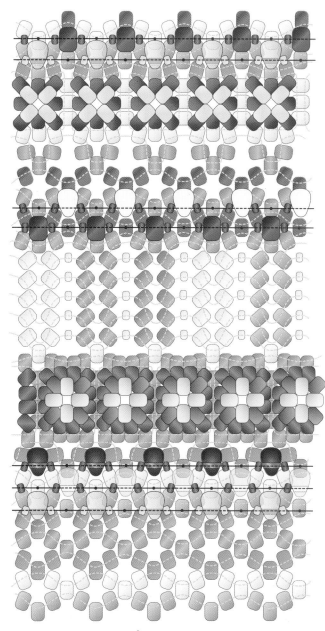

figure 14

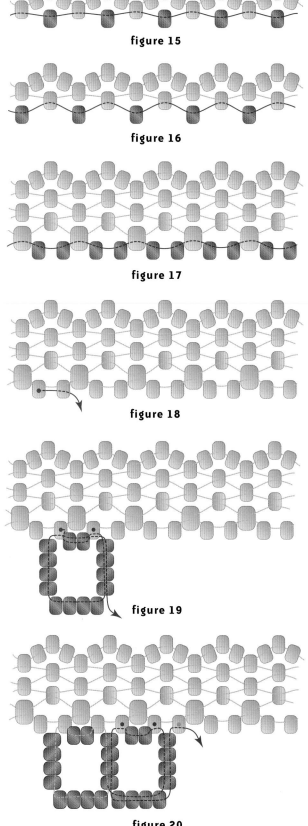

figure 15

figure 16

figure 17

figure 18

figure 19

figure 20

▶ Clasp Bead

You may use single thread and reinforce your work along the way or work with doubled thread. You'll work from the last round of netting completed on the tube.

Round 1 With the thread exiting any middle bead in a 3-drop netting unit, string one B and pass through the middle bead of the next unit. Repeat to add a total of five Bs (figure 15). Step down through the first B added.

Round 2 To work tubular peyote stitch, string one B and pass through the next B added in the previous round. Repeat to add a total of five Bs (figure 16). Step down through the first bead added in this round.

Round 3 Repeat round 2.

Round 4 Repeat round 2 with five 8° Js.

Round 5 Repeat round 2 using sets of two Bs as if they were one bead, adding 10 beads total (figure 17). Step down through the first two Bs added in this round (figure 18).

Round 6 Referring to figure 19, string two Bs and pass through one round 5 bead (red dot); string 12 Bs and pass through one round 5 bead (blue dot), the two Bs just added, one round 5 bead (red dot), and four Bs just added. Referring to figure 20, string eight Bs and pass through one bead in round 5 (red dot); string two Bs and pass through the next round 5 bead (blue dot), four beads from the previous unit, eight Bs just added, and the next round 5 bead (green dot). Referring to figure 21, string two Bs and pass through the next round 5 bead (red dot); string eight Bs and pass through four Bs from the previous unit and one round 5 bead (blue dot); pass through two beads just added, the next round 5 bead (red dot), and four Bs just added. Continue with modified right angle weave to complete five units (figure 22). Step down to exit four Bs on the leading edge of the round and the first B in the next set of four. **Note**: These units will be filled in later with 4-drop bumps.

Round 7 To work modified peyote stitch, string one J and pass through the fourth B in the current set of four edge beads and the first B in the next set of four edge beads. Repeat to add a total of five Js (figure 23). Step down through the first bead added.

Continued on page 56

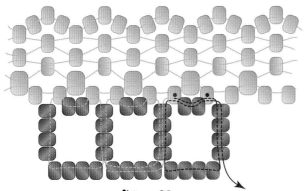

figure 21

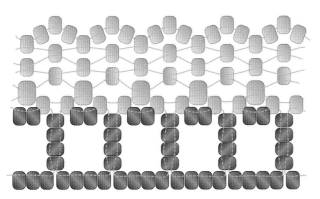

figure 22

**Color variations in
Softly (left) and High Times**

RIFF IT

• Work in a restricted color palette; for example, primarily matte black with smartly placed jet luster accents.

• Stitch 3-mm crystals in the netting ditch.

• Work a length two or more times longer and without the tube core.

• Work shorter, or flat, bumps. Or, stitch 5-mm beads or crystals in place of bumps.

• Work a short length and finish the necklace with strung beads or lengths of chain and a purchased clasp.

• Make the beadwork into a hatband.

• Modify the bead counts and, instead of making a necklace, cover a cylindrical wood needle case.

• Make a bangle length, closing the tube with colorful electrical tape or a peg that fits the inner diameter of the tubing. Bring the base ends together at any 3-drop netting row.

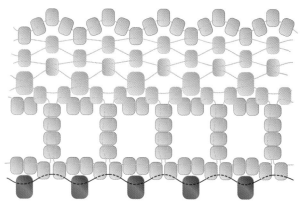

figure 23

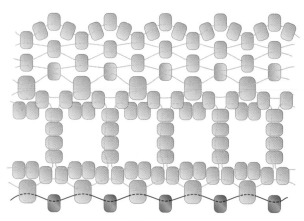

figure 24

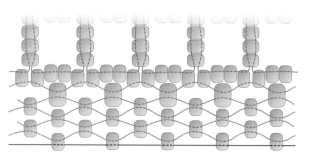

figure 25

figure 26

Round 8 To work tubular peyote stitch, string one B and pass through the next bead added in the previous round. Repeat to add a total of five Bs (figure 24). Step down through the first bead added.

Round 9 Repeat round 8.

Round 10 Repeat round 8 with five Fs.

Round 11 Repeat round 8 with five Es.

Cinch Without adding beads, pass through the five Es from round 11 twice and pull taut (figure 25). Weave in excess thread or use it to add the 4-drop bump as follows.

Add 4-Drop Bumps to Round 6

Add a 4-drop bump to each right angle weave unit made in round 6. Use Bs for rounds 1 and 2, Fs for round 3, and Es for round 4/cinch.

▶ Clasp Loop

Make a loop to accommodate the clasp button as outlined below. Work with a single thread and reinforce every stitch with a second pass. Reinforce the two points where the loop connects to the necklace as many times as the bead holes will allow. You'll work off the first round of netting at the beginning of the tube.

Rounds 1 and 2 Repeat rounds 1 and 2 of the clasp bead.

Round 3–5 Repeat round 2 of the clasp bead.

Round 6/Cinch Without adding beads, pass through the five Bs from round 5 twice. Pull the thread taut and exit from any B in the round.

▶ Add the Loop

This is a length of tubular peyote with only two beads in each row—a 1-drop bump. Reinforce each round before beginning the next round. Refer to figure 26 for rounds 1 and 2.

Round 1 String one H, pass back through the B just exited, string one H and pass back through the B and the first H added (red line).

Round 2 String one H and pass through the second H added in the previous round, string one H and pass through the first H added in the previous round. Step up through the first bead added in this round (blue line).

Repeat round 2 for 54 rows of tubular peyote stitch, alternating two rows of H and two rows of I. Secure the final row to the opposite B in the first round of netting on the tube. Weave in thread and trim excess.

JAZZ

You wear fancy clothes and tell folks what's on your mind. Being sassy and independent are prerequisites for stitching up and wearing a stunner like this. Enjoy living high on your nickels and dimes, and let the beads shimmy through your fingers. Just like the song says, "Jazz ain't got nothin' but soul."

SUPPLIES

Size 11° bronze round seed beads, 80 g

Size 6° light pink silver-lined round seed beads, 60 g

Size 8° bronze round seed beads, 80 g

280 light peach AB bicone crystals, 4 mm

4 gold closed jump rings, 4 mm

12 gold open jump rings, 4 mm

Supplies for beaded toggle, or a purchased clasp

Size 12 beading needles

Golden thread

Sharp snips

Suede or velvet work surface

TECHNIQUES

Right Angle Weave

Beaded Toggle Closure (optional)

Jump Rings

FINISHED SIZE

Each side, 15¼ inches (38.7 cm) long

Made in Nature Girl colorway

► Overview

First you'll use right angle weave to create a base of 8° round seed beads, then you'll embellish the base with 5-drop netting in 11° and 6° round seed beads and 4-mm bicone crystals. Finally, you'll finish with a custom beaded toggle or a purchased closure.

► Base

Following the schematic in figure 1, weave a 2-drop right angle weave base with 8°s. Pay careful attention to the turnarounds, which vary from row to row, to create the diagonal shape. Work with doubled thread for extra strength.

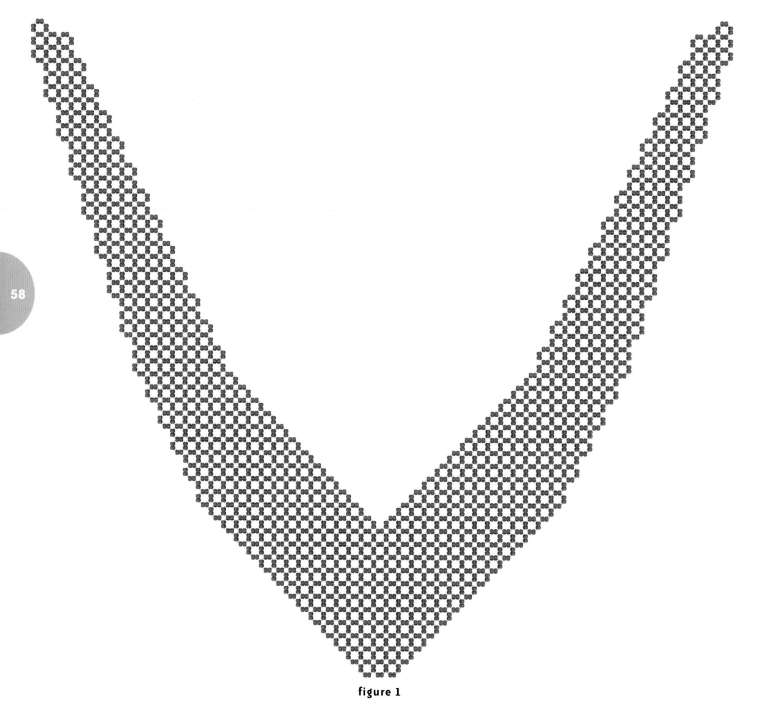

figure 1

▶ Embellishment

Following the instructions below and referring to figure 2, add vertical layers consisting of five rows of 5-drop netting. I like to begin at the center of the neckpiece and work toward the sides. Add the netting embellishment only to vertical units of B that have complete units to the left and right. Work with doubled thread for extra strength.

Row 1 With the thread exiting a base bead as shown with the red dot in figure 2, string five 11°s and pass through the bead next to the one first exited. *String five 11°s and pass through the second bead in the next set of two. Repeat from * nine times or to the end of the row (red line).

Row 2 String five 11°s and pass back through the third (middle) bead of the last net added in row 1. *String five 11°s and pass through the third bead of the next net in row 1. Repeat from * nine times or to the end of the row (blue line).

Row 3 String five 11°s and pass back through the third (middle) bead of the last net added in row 2. *String five 11°s and pass through the third bead of the next net in row 2. Repeat from * nine times or to the end of the row (green line).

Row 4 String two 11°s, one 6°, and two 11°s; pass back through the third (middle) bead of the last net added in row 3. *String two 11°s, one 6°, and two 11°s; pass through the third bead of the next net in row 3. Repeat from * nine times or to the end of the row (black line).

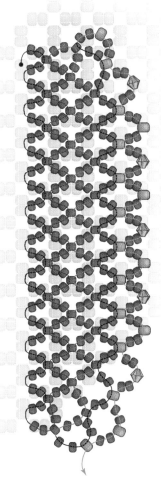

figure 2

The underside of the necklace

Row 5 String two 11°s, one 6°, and two 11°s; pass back through the 6° of the last net in row 4. *String two 11°s, one 4-mm bicone, and two 11°s; pass through the 6° of the next net in row 4. String two 11°s, one 6°, and two 11°s; pass through the 6° of the next net in row 4. Repeat from * four times or to the end of the row (gold line).

Weave down through the netting and the base to exit the lower bead on the opposite side of the right angle weave unit just embellished. Repeat rows 1 through 5 to embellish the entire length—in this case, you'll work one more unit than you did for the first sequence.

Continue in this manner to embellish the entire base.

figure 3

▶ Finish

To attach a 4-mm closed jump ring to each upper end of the base, weave through the beadwork to exit the first bead of the final unit of the base (figure 3, red line). String a 4-mm closed jump ring and pass through the second bead of the final unit and the remaining six beads of the same unit. Repeat the thread path to reinforce and weave through the neighboring unit for additional support.

Make a beaded toggle if desired. Attach it, or a purchased clasp, to the soldered jump rings with double jump ring connections. Use one set of double jump rings to attach the ring end and five sets to attach the bar end.

Color variation in Stagelight

RIFF IT

• Modify the base
to create a smaller
centerpiece and finish the
piece with heavy chain or beads
strung on flexible beading wire.

• To cut costs, use only 6° round
seed beads in the fifth row
of embellishing.

• Try the pattern with 11° s
and 15°s.

• Modify the base so it's
bracelet length.

Made in High Times colorway

NIGHT IN TUNISIA

The inimitable Dizzy Gillespie captured a sense of Mother Africa in 1942 when he wrote "Night in Tunisia." With its unique and mysterious feel, and even without Sarah Vaughan singing the lyrics, the melody has you on camelback, riding through fragrant, spice-infused twilight.

▶ Overview

The beadwork begins with a base of right angle weave, and the fun begins as the various size beads used to fill the units pull the 90° corners into 135° and 45° angles. You'll stitch around the perimeter and add dangles and chain along the way, then attach simple findings. The beadwork is approximately 4 inches (10.2 cm) wide. Refer to figure 1 (page 64) for all steps.

▶ Base

With A, stitch a right angle weave base with modified bead counts following the red line in the figure. You may begin at any point in the pattern, but be sure to follow the principles of right angle weave. To add an extra 16-bead unit to the center front, begin at the blue dot and exit four As of the center unit (blue dot, blue line); string 17 As, pass through them again—except the first A—string one A, and pass through the four As of the center front unit.

▶ 4-Drop Diagonal Bumps

Follow the instructions for 4-drop diagonal bumps but use the beads indicated below. Fill in all 25 of the 16-bead right angle weave units. There is no specified thread path for moving between the bumps.

Color variation in Nature Girl

SUPPLIES

Size 11° round seed beads:

A, hematite luster, 6 g

B, lavender AB, < 1 g

C, size 8° bronze metallic round seed beads, 2 g

Size 15° round seed beads

D, green silver-lined matte, < 1 g

E, hematite luster, < 1 g

F, 7 crystal bicones, cyclamen opal, 4 mm

G, 7 crystal sequins, cyclamen opal, 4 mm

H, 7 crystal rounds, cyclamen opal, 6 mm

16 inches (40.6 cm) of 2-mm cable chain

1 spring ring clasp, 5 mm

1 split ring, 5 mm

Size 12 beading needles

Gray thread

Sharp snips

Suede or velvet work surface

Chain-nose pliers

Wire cutter

TECHNIQUES

Right Angle Weave

4-Drop Diagonal Bump

FINISHED SIZE

4 inches (10.2 cm) at its widest point

Round 1 Two Bs and two Cs added alternately—with Cs on the left and right.

Round 2 Four Ds.

Cinch Pass two times through the Cs and the Ds.

► Edges and Dangles

With single thread, follow the green line in the illustration to pass through the outer-most beads for a finished look, adding dangles along the way. For each dangle string one E, one F, one G, one H, and one E, and pass back up the series to continue following the green line.

► Finish

Cut the chain into two 8-inch (20.3 cm) lengths. Weave in a new thread or use an existing one to stitch one end of each chain in the corners of the uppermost units, following the black line. Reinforce. Connect the spring ring clasp to the end of one chain. Twist the split ring onto the other chain end.

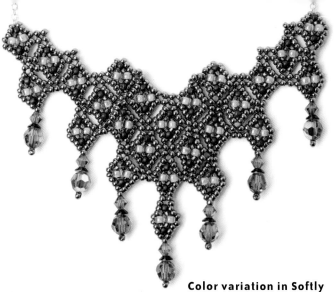

Color variation in Softly

64

figure 1

'ROUND MIDNIGHT

The influence of pianist and composer Thelonious Monk spread far and wide like a sweet smoky haze—a glimmer of his genius was even shed upon this pendant. Sparkling crystals mark the midnight hour's magic arrival.

Made in Softly colorway

SUPPLIES

Size 11° silver metallic round seed beads, 3 g

Size 15° silver metallic round seed beads, 1 g

12 crystal AB rose montées, 3.5 mm

Silver chain necklace, 18 inches (45.7 cm)

Size 12 beading needles

Gray thread

Sharp snips

Suede or velvet work surface

TECHNIQUES

Right Angle Weave

3/3/3/4-Drop Bump

Flat 3/3/3/4-Drop Bump

Finish with Montées

FINISHED SIZE

Ring, 1½ inches (3.8 cm) outer diameter

▶ Overview

You'll bead two circular bases in right angle weave with a single thread. The large units of the bases are embellished in different manners, and the two faces are stitched back-to-back and strung on a necklace chain.

▶ Bases (Make 2)

With a single thread, make a circular strip of right angle weave one unit by 24 units as outlined below. All steps for the base are shown in figure 1. Excess thread may be worked in and cut, or saved for embellishing or stitching the bases together. Stitch all units twice to reinforce them.

Unit 1 String ten 11°s and three 15°s, tie a simple double knot, and pass through the first three 11°s again.

Unit 2 String five 11°s and one 15°; pass through the three 11°s last exited and the five 11°s just added.

Unit 3 String three 15°s and seven 11°s; pass through the three 11°s last exited, then the three 15°s and the first three 11°s just added.

Repeat units 2 and 3 ten more times.

Unit 4 To join the circle, string two 11°s, pass through the three 11°s of unit 1, string one 15°, and pass through the three 11°s of the previous unit.

▶ Embellishment

Working with the large units, embellish the front base with 3-round bumps and montées, and fill the back base with 1-round flat bumps as follows.

Front Base Work a 3/3/3/4-drop bump on the first unit and cinch, then stitch a montée to the final round of the bump. Weave to the next large unit. Repeat 11 more times.

Back Base Work the first round of a flat 3/3/3/4-drop bump on the first unit and cinch. Weave to the next large unit. Repeat 11 more times.

▶ Connect the Bases

Working with single thread in right angle weave, stitch the outer edges of the front and back bases together with 11°s. To allow space for the necklace chain to be inserted through the beadwork, add two 11°s in the first and second sections but only one 11° to all subsequent sections (figure 2).

Join the inner edge as shown in figure 3, adding one 11° at a time.

▶ Finish

String one end of the necklace chain through the two-bead connection section.

This project also makes a nice brooch. Simply ditch the chain and stitch a bar pin to the back.

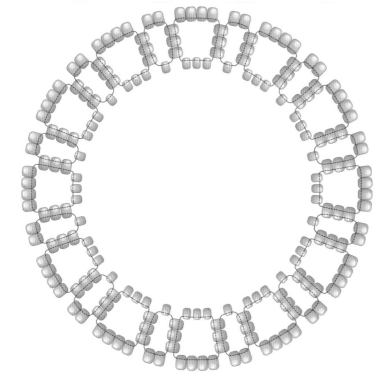

figure 1

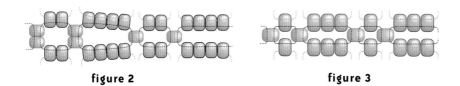

figure 2   **figure 3**

DROP ME OFF
IN HARLEM

**Nick Kenny's lyrics for Duke Ellington's 1933 tune "Drop Me Off in Harlem"
captured a classy uptown style—and so does this drop-shaped pendant.
The girl described in the song would have worn a twinkling
trinket just like this one for a night on the town.**

Made in Nature Girl colorway

SUPPLIES

Size 11° copper metallic round seed beads, 4 g

8 round sterling silver beads, 2 mm

7 crystal AB rose montées, 5 mm

1 crystal AB rose montée, 3.5 mm

Silver chain necklace, 18 inches (45.7 cm)

Size 12 beading needles

Apricot thread

Sharp snips

Suede or velvet work surface

TECHNIQUES

Right Angle Weave

2-Drop Bump

4-Drop Bump

Finish with Finial Beads

Finish with Montées

FINISHED SIZE

2¼ x 1½ inches (5.7 x 3.8 cm)

► Overview

For this necklace you'll stitch two right angle weave bases and embellish the top side of one base. Stitch the bases together and place them on a necklace chain.

► Base

Create two bases of modified right angle weave with seed beads as outlined below. Stitch all units twice to reinforce. Refer to figure 1 for steps 1 and 2 of the base and for steps 1 through 3 of the bumps and montées.

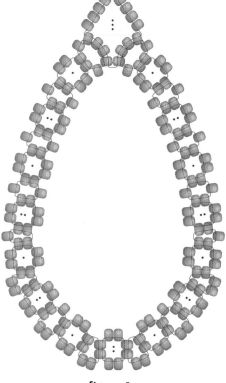

figure 1

1 Beginning with a unit below the eight beads shown at the center top in figure 1, work 31 units of modified right angle weave as illustrated, ending with the unit below the other side of the eight center beads.

2 After exiting the last bead of the last unit, close up the base by stringing eight beads as shown, passing through four beads of the first unit, and passing through four beads of the last unit added.

► Bumps and Montées

Use the seed beads to add bumps to one of the bases, then add montées as follows.

1 Add 2-drop bumps topped with a 2-mm sterling silver bead (finial bead) to the units marked with one red dot in figure 1.

2 Add a 5-mm rose montée to the units marked with two red dots in figure 1.

3 To the top eight-bead unit, add a 4-drop bump with 4 rows, cinch the four beads of the final row, and stitch the 3.5-mm rose montée to the cinched beads.

► Connect the Bases

Working in right angle weave, stitch the front and back bases together on both the inner and the outer edges; use single thread and, adding one bead at a time, stitch each unit twice. To create enough space for the necklace chain to be inserted through the beadwork, add two beads to the top unit but only one bead to all subsequent units (figure 2).

► Finish

Thread the necklace chain through the two larger openings at the top of the component.

figure 2

FLY ME
TO THE MOON

Without fail, Maria and Burt came around to listen to us play. They'd gotten together late in life and were living out their lives downtown—Burt with amazingly white hair, Maria in comfy cottons. They visited with us on breaks. After Maria was gone, Burt continued to request her favorite song, "Fly Me to the Moon." He'd nod his head and remember. This one's for her.

Made in High Times colorway

SUPPLIES

Size 11° round seed beads:

A, dark fuchsia matte, 2 g

B, opaque lavender AB, 5 g

C, yellow olive silver-lined, 20 g

17 emerald AB bicone crystals*, 4 mm

11 emerald AB round crystals*, 6 mm

1 plastic ring, 1½ inches (3.8 cm) in diameter

Size 12 beading needles

Apricot thread

Sharp snips

Suede or velvet work surface

* Select a crystal color that contrasts with A, B, and C—maybe even something a little unexpected.

TECHNIQUES

Right Angle Weave

Beaded Toggle Closure (optional)

Bead Caps

Tubular Peyote Stitch

FINISHED SIZE

Rope, 36 inches (91.4 cm) long

Pendant, 4½ inches (11.4 cm) long

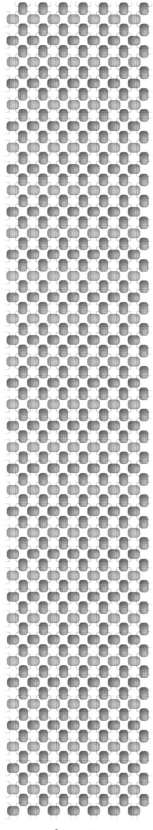

▶ Overview

A plastic ring is covered with 1-drop right angle weave worked in a continuous tube, then fringed with lengths of 1-drop tubular peyote stitch. Tubular peyote stitch also forms the necklace length, which incorporates crystals and stitched bead caps. Use thin thread and reinforce all stitches.

▶ Centerpiece

With A and B work 37 rows of 1-drop right angle weave in a tube around the ring following the color pattern in figure 1. Close the tube by adding one more row of seven Bs one at a time. For a tidy appearance and additional strength, stitch each unit twice before adding the next unit.

▶ Bead Caps

Using B, make seventeen bead caps, then set them aside.

▶ Fringe

Following the instructions below, use Cs to work rings with drop lengths of tubular peyote stitch coming off them. Add accent beads at the bottom of each drop length.

Rings (Make 5)

Work 34 rounds of 4-bead 1-drop tubular peyote stitch, stitching each round twice before adding the next round. Wrap the length around the centerpiece and connect the final round to the first round, reinforcing the thread path.

figure 1

Drop Lengths

With the thread exiting any bead of the ring, string one C and pass through a bead two rounds away. String one C and pass through the first bead exited again. Repeat the thread path (figure 2, red line).

Continue to work 1-drop tubular peyote stitch for a total of 40 rounds for the two shortest fringes, a total of 46 rounds for the two medium fringes, and a total of 52 rounds for the longest fringe.

Accent Beads

Exiting an end C, string one B, one 4-mm bicone, one bead cap, one 6-mm round, and one B. Pass back up through all the accent beads except the last B added and through the other end C. Pass back down through the accent beads and back up and through the first C (figure 3). Repeat until the accent beads are secure. Repeat at the ends of all the drop lengths.

▶ Necklace

Now make a rope of 4-bead 1-drop tubular peyote and accent beads to connect to the centerpiece with two rings as follows. The rope has six short lengths of 1-drop tubular peyote and one long length.

Rings (Make Two)

With C, make rings and attach them to the centerpiece as for the fringe.

Short Lengths

With the thread exiting any C of a ring, work as for the fringe drop length for 20 rounds.

Weave in the thread ends. Repeat on the second ring.

Work four more lengths of 4-bead 1-drop tubular peyote stitch 20 rounds long. Weave in the thread ends.

Long Length

Using C, work a length of 4-bead 1-drop tubular peyote 20 inches (50.8 cm) long to make up the remaining length of the necklace.

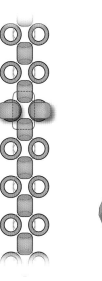

figure 2   **figure 3**

figure 4

Accents

With the thread exiting a bead at the end of one drop length attached to the centerpiece, string one C, one 4-mm bicone, one bead cap, one 6-mm round, one bead cap, one 4-mm bicone, and one C; pass through a bead at the end of a separate short length. Pass back through the accent beads and through the other bead at the end of the attached length. Pass back through the accent beads to the other bead at the end of the added length. Repeat until the accent beads are secure. Weave in the thread ends (figure 4).

Repeat this process, adding one more short length, the long length, and the three remaining short lengths, attaching the last short length to the other ring around the centerpiece.

Colorway variations in Softly (left) and Stagelight

RIFF IT

• To make earrings, stitch a closed ring attached to an ear wire to the first fringe row.

• Make a bracelet, or even an anklet, by connecting a shorter peyote stitch length between the sections of accents.

• Shorten or lengthen the fringe and lengths.

• Add more fringe, or none at all.

CHAPTER THREE
RINGS AND EARRINGS

Made in Blue in Green colorway

GROOVE

Every moment of a live jazz performance is a chance to hear musicians reach new heights. Drummer Billy Higgins softly grunting with the beat. Pianist Keith Jarrett vocalizing an unintelligible song. These are the moments when a musician goes deep into a tune and syncs with other band members—the times when they all find their groove.

▶ Overview

You'll make a right angle weave base, close the ends with smaller embellished units, embellish the large units, and attach the components to ear wires.

▶ Base

Using A and B, work a three-row tube of right angle weave in varying drop counts following the instructions below and referring to figure 1. For a tidy appearance and additional strength, stitch each unit again before adding the next unit.

Round 1 String 16 As, tie a double overhand knot, and pass through the first four beads just strung. *String one B, four As, and one B, then pass through the last four As exited, the B just added, and the four As just added. String 12 As, then pass through the last four As exited and the first eight As just added. Repeat from * two times. String one B, pass through four As from the first unit, string one B, and pass through the last four As exited (red line).

Weave through the beadwork to exit any set of four As on an open edge.

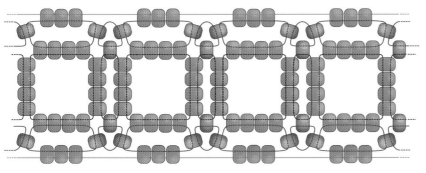

figure 1

SUPPLIES

Size 11° round seed beads:

A, olive opaque matte AB, < 1 g

B, bronze metallic, < 1 g

C, light yellow silver-lined AB, < 1 g

D, blue zircon silver-lined, < 1 g

26 gold-filled round beads, 2 mm

2 gold-filled 20-gauge closed jump rings, 4 mm

1 pair of gold-filled lever-back ear wires with open loops

Size 12 beading needles

Blue thread

Sharp snips

Suede or velvet work surface

Chain-nose pliers

TECHNIQUES

Right Angle Weave

4-Drop Bump

3-Drop Bump

Finish with Finial Beads

Jump Rings

FINISHED SIZE

Each bead, 7/8 x 7/8 inch (2.2 x 2.2 cm)

Round 2 String one B, three As, and one B, then pass through the last four As exited and the first B just added. *String one B, pass through one B from round 1, the last B exited, the B just added, and four As from round 1. String one B and three As; pass through the last B added, four As from round 1, and the B just added. Repeat from * two times. Pass through the next B in round 2, the B in round 1, and the last B exited (blue line).

Cinch Pass through four sets of three As on the outer edge. Repeat the thread path and pull taut (green line).

Weave through the beadwork to exit four As on the other open edge. Repeat round 2 and cinch.

▶ Bumps

Stitch a 4-drop bump with three rounds to each 4-drop right angle weave unit. Use C for round 1, D for round 2, and B for round 3/cinch.

Stitch a 3-drop bump with only two rounds to each 3-drop right angle weave opening. Use D for round 1 and B for round 2/cinch.

▶ Finish

Add a 2-mm gold-filled finial bead to the top of each 4-drop bump, to the bottommost 3-drop bump, and to each three-bead unit of B (figure 2).

Stitch a closed jump ring to the final row of the topmost 3-drop bump. Attach an ear wire loop to the jump ring with chain-nose pliers.

Repeat all steps to make a second earring.

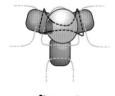

figure 2

76

BILLIE

This project is a simple tribute to an icon of jazz history. Billie Holiday was known for a vocal style heavily influenced by jazz instrumentalists, for the gardenias in her hair, and for her challenging life. She could well have worn this ring upon a gloved finger.

Made in Blue in Green colorway

SUPPLIES

Size 11° medium green matte metallic AB round seed beads, 2 g

16 rose montées, 5 mm

2 rose montées, 3.5 mm

Size 12 beading needles

Blue thread

Sharp snips

Suede or velvet work surface

TECHNIQUES

Right Angle Weave

Montées to 2-Drop Right Angle Weave

Finish with Montées

Flat 3-Drop Bump

FINISHED SIZE

Top of ring, ⅝ inch (1.6 cm) in diameter

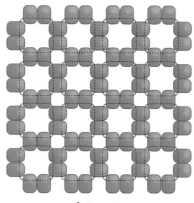

figure 1

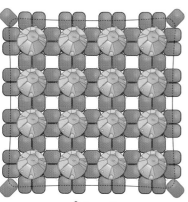

figure 2

78

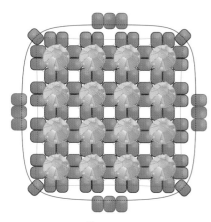

figure 3

▶ Overview

A flat piece of right angle weave is embellished with montées and cinched into a ball, and a flat strip of modified right angle weave makes the band.

▶ Ball

Base Using single thread and size 11° seed beads, work a 2-drop right angle weave piece that is four units wide and four units tall (figure 1).

Embellish Stitch 5-mm montées to all 16 units on one side, then pass through sets of two beads on the edge and add one seed bead at each corner (figure 2). Pull up the slack so the beadwork becomes a ball. Reinforce along the red line shown in the figure several times. Exit through any corner bead.

Cinch String three seed beads and pass through the next corner bead from the previous step. Repeat three more times to add a total of 12 beads (figure 3). Reinforce

along the red line shown in the figure. Exit through the last bead in any set of three beads just added.

▶ Band

Work a length of modified right angle weave and fill it in to make flat to slightly cupped bumps as follows.

Base String nine seed beads, pass through the last three beads exited (three beads on the ball the first time) and the first six beads just added. Reinforce with a second pass. String five beads, then pass through the last three beads exited and the first four beads just added (figure 4). Reinforce with a second pass. Repeat from the beginning of the step to the desired length, ending with a large unit and passing through the three beads on the other side of the ball.

Bumps Fill in the large units with flat 3-drop bumps.

Accent Stitch 3.5-mm rose montées to the two bumps closest to the ball.

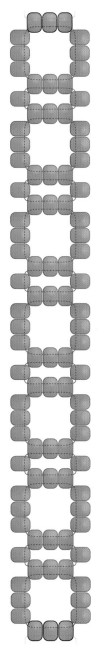

figure 4

Color variations in Stagelight (left) and Softly

NIGHTINGALE

The popular British song "A Nightingale Sang in Berkeley Square" came out in 1939 and later made its way into the standard jazz songbook. The moonlight over the star-paved plaza promises romantic affairs. Is it true love, or a passing fling? These questions fade as the greats—Carmen McRae, Nat King Cole—play the song's sparkling notes.

Made in High Times colorway

SUPPLIES

232 lavender round crystals, 2 mm

8 size 11° green iris metallic round seed beads

62 sterling silver round beads, 2 mm

2 crystal AB rose montées, 3.5 mm

2 sterling silver closed jump rings, 4 mm

1 pair of sterling silver ear wires, 1½ inches (3.8 cm) long

Size 12 beading needles

Lilac thread

Sharp snips

Suede or velvet work surface

Chain-nose pliers

TECHNIQUES

Right Angle Weave

Montée to 1-Drop Right Angle Weave

Ditch Beads

FINISHED SIZE

Components, each ⅝ inch (1.6 cm) square

► Overview

For each earring you'll stitch two 1-drop right angle weave bases together, add embellishment and a jump ring, then attach the component to an ear wire.

► Base

Steps 1 through 4 are shown in figure 1.

1 With a single thread, work a base of 1-drop right angle weave of 2-mm crystals that is five units square (right side, red line).

2 Repeat step 1, but make the center unit of the base with 11°s (left side, red line).

3 Join the bases by adding a final row of 2-mm rounds on three edges (blue line).

4 Join the fourth edge but in one corner add a closed jump ring in place of a bead (green line).

► Embellishment

Stitch a rose montée to the 11°-bead center unit of the front base. Stitch in the ditch along the line between the outer and the next inside right angle weave units with 2-mm rounds (red dots in figure 1).

Open the ear wire loop with chain-nose pliers, slip through the jump ring, and close the loop.

Repeat all steps to make a second earring.

Colorway variations, both in Stagelight

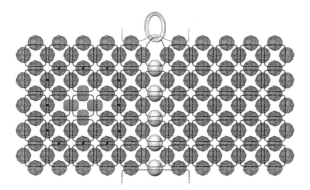

figure 1

Made in Softly colorway

FIVE-PIECE BAND

Jazz combos can be assembled in endless ways; so can beads. Like the sweet vibrato and glissando tunes of a sugar band, montées and stitches come together for these four stackable rings.

▶ Overview

With a single thread and 11° seed beads, you'll work units of right angle weave and a length of square stitch, then embellish the right angle weave portion of the base with bumps, rose montées, or chaton montées. *Note*: It's exceptionally nice to work this pattern up while listening to Dave Brubeck's 1959 recording of Paul Desmond's "Take Five."

In the photo above, variation 1 is shown at the top. Below it are variations 2 and 4, with variation 3 at the bottom.

SUPPLIES

Variation 1:
  Size 11° metallic silver round
  seed beads, < 1 g

Variation 2:
  Size 11° metallic silver round
  seed beads, < 1 g
  5 crystal AB chaton montées, 5 mm

Variation 3:
  Size 11° metallic silver round
  seed beads, 1 g
  5 crystal AB chaton montées, 5 mm

Variation 4:
  Size 11° metallic silver round
  seed beads, < 2 g
  5 crystal AB chaton montées, 5 mm

All variations:
  Size 12 beading needles

  Gray thread

  Sharp snips

  Suede or velvet work surface

TECHNIQUES

Right Angle Weave

Montée to 2-Drop Right Angle Weave

2-Drop Bump

Finish with Finial Beads

FINISHED SIZE

Dimensions vary

figure 1

▶ Base

Work a base of right angle weave and square stitch for all variations as follows. Both steps are illustrated in figure 1.

Right Angle Weave Length Work five units of 2-drop right angle weave, reinforcing each unit before adding the next one (red line). End with the thread exiting the two beads at the bottom of the strip.

Square Stitch Length String two beads and pass through the last two beads

exited and the two beads just added. Pass through all four beads again to reinforce. Repeat to desired ring size (blue line). Join the square stitch length to the other end of the right angle weave piece.

▶ Bumps and Finishing
Variation 1:
2-drop bumps with finials

Add 2-drop bumps to each of the five openings of the 2-drop right angle weave of the base. Top each bump with a finial bead.

Variation 2:
chatons without riser

Stitch 5-mm chaton montées to each of the five openings of the 2-drop right angle weave of the base.

Variation 3:
chatons with 1-bead riser

With the thread exiting from two beads at one side of the base, add units of 2/1 right angle weave to both sides of the base (figure 2).

Working in right-angle weave, add two beads at a time to close the strip, reinforcing as you go (figure 3, red line). Close up the units at the ends (blue line). Stitch 5-mm chaton montées to each of the five openings of the 2-drop right angle weave of the riser.

Variation 4:
chatons with 2-bead riser

With the thread exiting from two beads at the side of the base, add units of 2-drop right angle weave to both sides of the base (figure 4).

Working in right angle weave, add two beads at a time to close the top, reinforcing as you go (figure 5, red line). Close up the units at the ends (blue line). Stitch 5-mm chaton montées to each of the five openings of the 2-drop right angle weave of the riser.

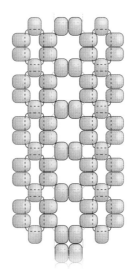

figure 2

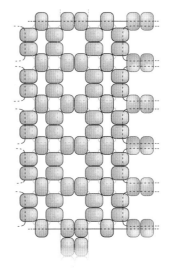

figure 3

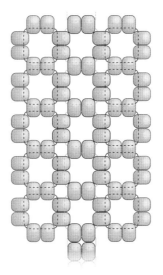

figure 4

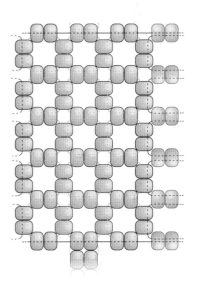

figure 5

RIFF IT

These will work with any variation.

• Add 1-drop bumps higher than one row and finish with 3.5-mm rose montées.

• Stitch 3-mm round or bicone beads into the 2-drop right angle weave.

• Stack the rings in different combinations for more or less sparkle.

Made in High Times colorway

SASSY

She grew up in Newark, New Jersey, and eventually became known as "Sassy" and "The Divine One." Sarah Vaughan was an American jazz singer who is especially close to my heart. These earrings are dedicated to her.

▶ Overview

You'll build three different size bumps on a right angle weave base, add a bead loop, attach an ear wire, and repeat. You'll begin by beading the largest unit and work your way up to the smallest unit. Work with a single thread. Reinforce all work. Figure 1 shows the right angle weave units and the added loop.

▶ Base

Using a single thread, string 20 As, tie a simple double knot to form a circle, and pass through the first five beads strung. Following the bead counts and red line in figure 1, work a base of right angle weave with As.

figure 1

SUPPLIES

A, size 11° lavender AB round seed beads, 2 g

Size 15° round seed beads:

    B, avocado matte AB, < 1 g

    C, maroon iris metallic, < 1 g

1 pair of silver lever-back ear wires with open loop

Size 12 beading needles

Lilac thread

Sharp snips

Suede or velvet work surface

Chain-nose pliers

TECHNIQUES

Right Angle Weave

5-Drop Bump

3/4/5/4-Drop Bump

3-Drop Bump

FINISHED SIZE

Beadwork, 1¼ inches (3.2 cm) long

**The back of
the earrings**

▶ Bumps

Stitch three different sizes of bumps up from the base as follows.

5-Drop Bumps

This bump is worked on the largest right angle weave unit. Using the bead types indicated below, make a 5-drop bump and cinch the beads in round 6.

Round 1 8A.

Round 2 8A.

Round 3 8B.

Round 4 8B.

Round 5 4B.

Round 6 4C.

3/4/5/4-Drop Bumps

This bump is worked on the middle right angle weave unit. Use the bead types indicated below and cinch the beads in round 4.

Round 1 5A.

Round 2 5A.

Round 3 5B.

Round 4 5C.

3-Drop Bumps

This bump is worked on the smallest unit at the top of the base using bead types indicated below. Cinch the beads in round 3.

Round 1 4A.

Round 2 4B.

Round 3 4C.

Loop

Following the blue thread path in figure 1, add a six-bead loop of Bs to the top of the base. Repeat the thread path two more times to secure.

▶ Finish

Use chain-nose pliers to open the ear wire loop, slide the ear wire loop over the six-bead loop, and close the ear wire loop.

Repeat all steps to make a second earring.

**Color variations in Nature Girl
(top) and Stagelight**

RIFF IT

• Make a bracelet by working the series of bumps long enough to encircle the wrist, and attach a clasp.

• Make one component and attach it to a chain for a simple pendant.

• Make a number of components, attach a closed ring to the loop of each, and string them on flexible beading wire with 4-mm crystal beads between them.

• Hang the components from hoop earrings instead of ear wires.

CHAPTER FOUR

BRACELETS

Made in High Times colorway

BIRTH OF THE COOL

In 1948, nine musicians convened in the New York apartment of composer and arranger Gil Evans and eventually made one of the most notable recordings in jazz history. Each musician brought a unique sound and ability to the group, which would record "Birth of the Cool" as the Miles Davis Nonet. This piece is named for their accomplishment—it's proof that wonderful things come in sets of nine.

▶ Overview

The bracelet starts with a base of right angle weave to which layers of beads in peyote stitch and right angle weave are added. Add to that embellishments of drops and montées, and finish with a multistrand clasp.

▶ Base

With A and B, work with a single thread and follow the color pattern in figure 1 to work a strip of right angle weave nine units wide and as long as needed. Begin with a section of A, work to desired length, and return to the first end to add rows of B as needed.

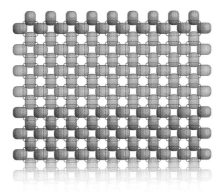

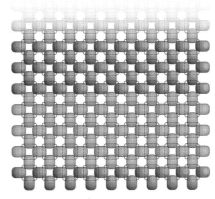

figure 1

SUPPLIES

Size 11° round seed beads:

A, light lavender matte AB, 11 g

B, maroon metallic iris, 4 g

C, burnt sienna opaque, 2 g

54 peridot silver-lined drop beads, 3.4 mm

36 crystal AB rose montées, 5 mm

6 liquid silver tubes, 5 mm

5-strand silver tube clasp, 32 mm

12 open silver 20-gauge jump rings, 4 mm

Size 12 beading needles

Lilac thread

Sharp snips

Suede or velvet work surface

Flush cutters

Chain-nose pliers

TECHNIQUES

Right Angle Weave

Ditch Beads

Montée to 1-Drop Right Angle Weave

Liquid Silver

Jump Rings

FINISHED SIZE

1 x 7 inches (2.5 x 17.8 cm)

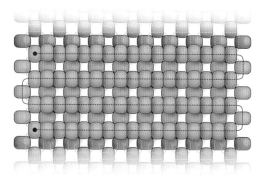

figure 2

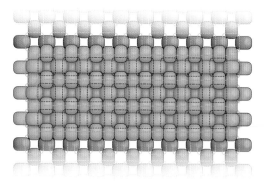

figure 3

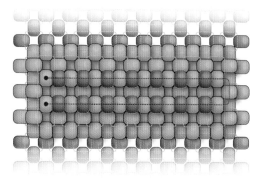

figure 4

figure 5

▶ **Layers**

Add layers of beadwork as follows. Passes 1 through 4 of layer 1 are shown in figure 2.

Layer 1, Pass 1 With the thread exiting an end bead in the first base row of A (red dot), add ditch beads by stringing one A and passing through the next A with the hole facing the same direction. Repeat seven more times. At the end of pass 1, pass through the next two beads in the right angle weave unit.

Layer 1, Passes 2–4 Repeat pass 1, ending at the blue dot in figure 2.

Layer 1, Passes 5–7 With the thread exiting an A at the beginning of pass 4, use the As added in the previous step as the top and bottom beads of right angle weave units and add one A at a time to complete the units (figure 3). Repeat to add a total of 27 A beads.

Layer 2, Passes 1 and 2 With the thread exiting either layer 1 bead shown with a red dot in figure 4, string one C and pass through the next A from layer 1 with the hole facing the same direction. Repeat six more times. Pass through the next two As in the right angle weave unit at the end of pass 1 and work pass 2 in the other direction.

Layer 2, Pass 3 With the thread exiting a C at the end of the last pass added, use the Cs added in the previous step as the top and bottom beads of right angle weave units and add one C at a time to complete the units (figure 5). Repeat to add a total of eight Cs.

Repeat all layering steps on each section of A beads on the base.

▶ Accents

Add rows of drops, seed beads, and montées to each layered section as outlined below. Rows 1 through 3 are shown in figure 6. Work with a doubled thread or reinforce your work—this area will rub against fabric and other surfaces.

Row 1 With the thread exiting any bead shown with a red dot, string one B and pass through the next A in the first layer with a hole facing the same direction—if you begin with a bead on the left, stitch to the right; if you begin with a bead on the right, stitch to the left. String one drop and pass through the next A in the same manner. Repeat to add a total of four Bs and three drops, finishing at the opposite end. Weave through the beadwork to exit the closest red dot.

Row 2 Repeat row 1.

Row 3 Add montées to every other right angle weave unit of layer 2.

Repeat all accent steps on all layered sections.

▶ Finish

Cut the second and fourth rings from both clasp ends with flush cutters. Stitch three liquid silver tubes to each end of the beadwork as shown in figure 7; reinforce the thread path. Attach the liquid silver tubes to the clasp loops with two jump rings each. Push play to enjoy your "Birth of the Cool" CD.

RIFF IT

• Work more or fewer than nine units across.

• Add tubular peyote stitch to the layers and finish with 3.5-mm rose montées.

• Layer in different bead colors.

• Make a series of short base lengths and connect them into a necklace.

• Make a square segment for a pendant.

• Add 3-mm bicones instead of montées, or daggers instead of drops.

• Work flat peyote stitch off the right angle weave edges.

• Layer the entire piece.

• Add 11°s in place of drop beads and work them into a peyote stitch ruffle.

Colorway variation in Softly

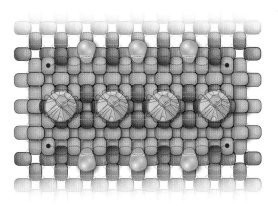

figure 6

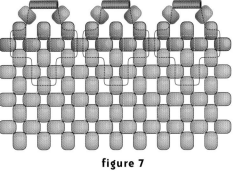

figure 7

Made in Stagelight colorway

FOUR

Eddy "Cleanhead" Vinson wrote the music to a blazing tune that Miles Davis made famous; my all-time favorite tune to sing, it's called "Four." With lyrics by Eddie Jefferson, the climax purports that the four greatest things in life are "truth, honor, and happiness, and one thing more, meaning only wonderful, wonderful love, that'll make it four." This project is all about the number four—four bumps, four contrast colors, four sets of jump rings, and more.

▶ Overview

You'll create a series of components in right angle weave with liquid silver connecting points, and then link the components to each other and to the clasp ends with jump rings. Work with a single thread for the entire project. *Note:* Stitch the base first, then add the first set of connecting points, then the first bump. Add the second set of connecting points, then the second bump, and so on. Adding the connecting points before the bumps ensures that there will be enough room inside the beads to stitch everything in. Reinforce each row of bumps, if possible.

▶ Base

Follow the instructions below and refer to figure 1 to stitch a series of seven units in right angle weave with A and B—four large units and three small units.

Unit 1 Leaving a 6-inch (15.2 cm) tail, string 16 As and tie them into a ring with a simple double knot, then pass through the first four As strung.

Unit 2 String one B, four As, and one B; pass through the four As last exited, one B, and the four As just added.

Unit 3 String 12 As and pass through the four As last exited and the first eight As just added.

Repeat units 2 and 3 two more times.

Repeat all steps to make a total of 14 components.

figure 1

SUPPLIES

Size 11° round seed beads:

A, black matte, 20 g

B, fuchsia silver-lined matte, 2 g

C, silver, 2 g

D, ruby silver-lined AB, 2 g

E, bronze metallic, 2 g

F, yellow sparkle-lined crystal luster, 2 g

112 liquid silver tubes, 5 mm

120 open silver 20-gauge jump rings, 4 mm

7-strand silver sliding multistrand clasp, 41 mm

Size 12 beading needles

Gray thread

Sharp snips

Suede or velvet work surface

Chain-nose pliers

Flush wire cutters

TECHNIQUES

Right Angle Weave

Liquid Silver

4-Drop Bump

Jump Rings

FINISHED SIZE

1½ x 8 inches (3.8 x 20.3 cm)

► Connecting Points and Bumps

1 Following the thread path in figure 2, add one liquid silver tube flanked by two As on each side of the top large right angle weave unit of the first component. Reinforce the thread path.

2 Add a 4-drop bump to the unit with the connecting point. Use A for all beads in rounds 1 through 3, and work the last round of bumps with C.

3 Repeat steps 1 and 2 to add connecting points and bumps to the remaining three large units in the first component, working the last rounds of the bumps with D, E, and F respectively.

4 Repeat steps 1 through 3 to add connecting points and bumps to all 14 components, working the final round of bumps in the colors specified below.

Components 1, 5, 9, and 13: C, D, E, F.

Components 2, 6, 10, and 14: F, C, D, E.

Components 3, 7, and 11: E, F, C, D.

Components 4, 8, and 12: D, E, F, C.

figure 2

► Connections

Connect the first component to the second component with two jump rings around the liquid silver tubes at each connection point. (Use chain-nose pliers to open and close the jump rings.) Continue until all 14 components are connected, taking care that the components are in sequence.

► Clasp

With the flush part of the wire cutters against the main part of the clasp, remove the second, fourth, and sixths loops from both ends of the clasp. Connect one end of the clasp to the first component with two jump rings around the loops of the clasp and the liquid silver tubes of the component. Connect the other end to the final component in the same manner.

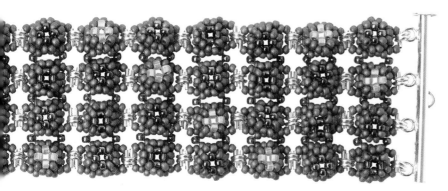

Colorway variations in Blue in Green (above) and Softly

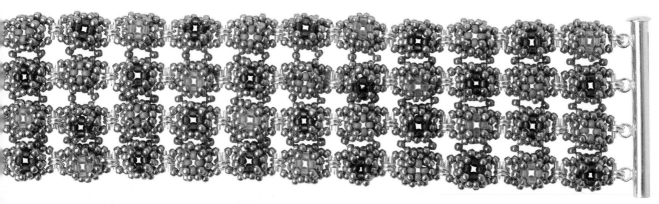

SWING TIME

With succinctly placed emphasis on just the right beat, jazz musicians give their edgy music a feel all its own. The distinctive style of swing jazz, with its lilting rhythm and soloists improvising over the melody, was the danceable style of bandleaders like Benny Goodman and Count Basie.

Made in Stagelight colorway

SUPPLIES

Size 11° round seed beads:

A, silver metallic, 12 g

B, red silver-lined, 15 g

C, dark gray matte, 15 g

8 liquid silver beads, 5 mm

7-strand silver sliding multistrand clasp, 41 mm

16 open silver 20-gauge jump rings, 4 mm

Size 12 beading needles

Gray, light gray, and red threads

Sharp snips

Suede or velvet work surface

Flush wire cutters

Chain-nose pliers

TECHNIQUES

Right Angle Weave

1-Drop Bump

Liquid Silver

Jump Rings

FINISHED SIZE

1⁷/₈ x 7⁵/₈ inches (4.7 x 20 cm)

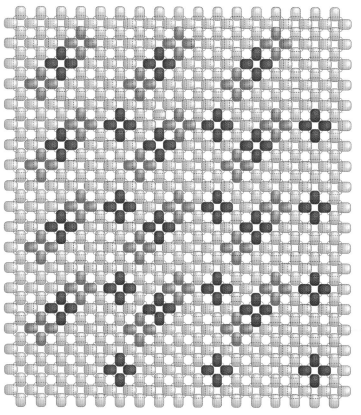

figure 1

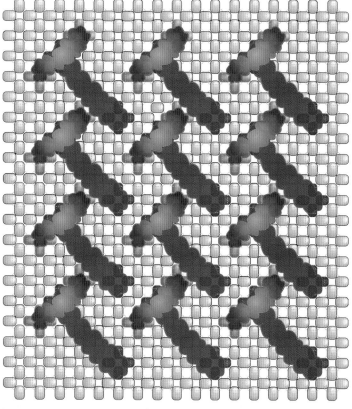

figure 2

▶ Overview

First you'll create a three-color right angle weave base, then add bumps, and finish with a multistrand clasp. **Tip:** Consider using up to three different thread colors if the bead colors contrast greatly, or use medium gray thread throughout.

▶ Base

Using A, B, C, and single thread, work a 17-unit-wide right angle weave base to the desired length following the pattern in figure 1. Begin at the top of the pattern, repeat to length, and finish with the pattern at the bottom. **Note**: The pattern repeat is four units long. The sample bracelet is 7½ inches (19 cm) long and the four-unit pattern is worked 14 times, followed by the last three-unit pattern.

▶ Bumps

Refer to figure 2 for the bump pattern.

With the thread exiting the bottom bead of the top left color B unit, work a 1-drop bump for 13 rows. Stitch the last row to the next B unit below and to the right on the base. Repeat to connect all pairs of B units.

With the thread exiting the bottom bead of the top left color C unit, work a 1-drop bump for 13 rows. Stitch the last row to the next C unit below and to the left on the base. Repeat to connect all pairs of C units.

▶ Clasp

Stitch four liquid silver beads flanked with As on each end of the base (figure 3). With the flush wire cutters, remove the second, fourth, and sixth loops from both parts of the clasp. Using chain-nose pliers, apply a double jump ring connection to all four points on each end between the bracelet and the clasp.

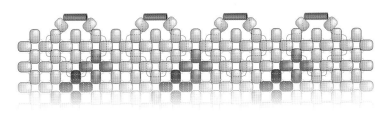

figure 3

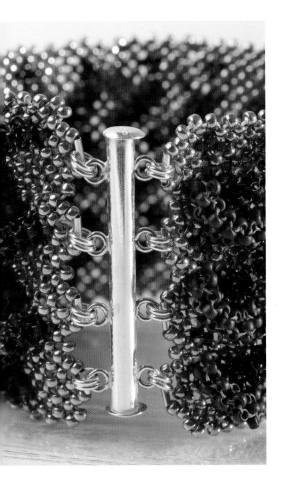

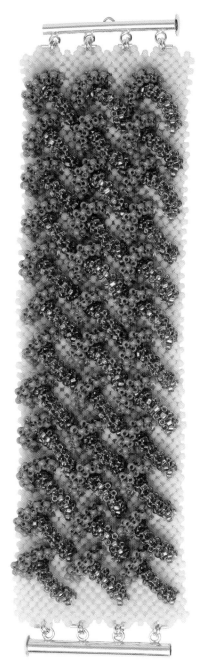

Color variations in Nature Girl (left) and High times

COCKTAILS FOR TWO

Big-band tunes conjure sophistication and romance. As sung by Ray Charles and Betty Carter on their self-titled 1961 duet album, "Cocktails for Two" overflows with affection and innuendo. This bracelet is the perfect accessory for cocktails enjoyed "in some secluded rendezvous, that overlooks the avenue."

Made in Stagelight colorway

SUPPLIES

Size 11° round seed beads:

A, black matte, 5 g

B, black luster, 5 g

C, bronze metallic, 5 g

Size 15° round seed beads:

D, ruby silver-lined AB, 5 g

E, bronze metallic, 2 g

138 bronze metallic drop seed beads, 3.4 mm

23 crystal AB chaton or rose montées, 3.5 mm

20-gauge silver jump rings, 4 mm:

4 closed

4 open

2 silver lobster clasps

2 silver split rings, 6 mm

Size 12 beading needles

Black thread

Sharp snips

Suede or velvet work surface

Chain-nose pliers

TECHNIQUES

Tubular Peyote Stitch

Right Angle Weave

Montée to 1-Drop Right Angle Weave

Jump Rings

FINISHED SIZE

1½ x 8 inches (3.8 x 20.3 cm)

► Overview

A series of peyote rings are connected with right angle weave bridges, then embellished with 15° seed beads, drop beads, and montées. You'll finish the piece with findings. **Note**: It may be difficult to know how many components you'll need for your own custom length, so work fewer than you think you'll need and add more later if necessary.

► Rings

Following the instructions below, work with single thread to stitch lengths of 4-bead 1-drop peyote stitch, and then join the ends to form rings. Always reinforce the row before the step up. Make eight rings each with A and B. Four possible connecting points are marked with red dots in figure 1. The rings at the bracelet ends will be bridged at two connecting points, and the remaining rings will be bridged at three connecting points.

Rounds 1 through 4 are shown in figure 2. Beginning a ring can be tricky. I like to pinch a bead from round 1 (shown with a red dot) with the tips of my thumb and index finger until the tube is four rounds long.

Rounds 1 and 2 String four As. Leaving a 6-inch (15.2 cm) tail, tie a simple double knot to form a ring and pass through the first A again (red line).

Round 3 String one A, skip one A, and pass through the next A (blue line).

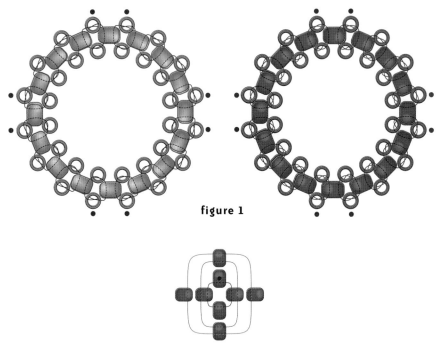

figure 1

figure 2

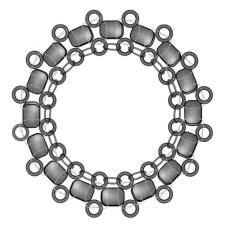

figure 3

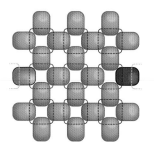

figure 4

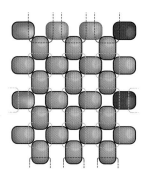

figure 5

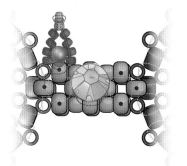

figure 6

Repeat once more and step up by passing through the first A added in the round.

Round 4 Repeat round 3 (green line).

Repeat to make 16 rounds. Stitch the final round to the first round securely.

Cinch With the thread exiting a bead on the ring's interior, pass through the next interior bead. Then go through the bead just exited, the interior bead a second time, the last bead exited, and the interior bead a third time. Pass through the next interior bead and repeat around the ring, pulling up the slack as you progress. The interior beads are linked together and cinched to refine the ring (figure 3). Weave in the remaining thread or save it for adding bridges.

▶ **Bridges**

Bridges of 1-drop right angle weave worked with single thread in a square-shaped tube connect the rings. Reinforce each 1-drop unit before adding the next unit. A rings will connect with a bridge to B rings and vice versa. Steps 1 and 2 are shown in figure 4.

1 With the thread exiting a connecting bead of an A ring, string three Cs and pass through the last bead exited and the first two beads added. String three Cs and pass through the last bead exited and the first two beads just added. String one C, pass through a connecting bead of a B ring, string one C, and pass through the last C exited from the previous unit and the first C added in this unit (red lines).

2 Continuing with 1-drop right angle weave, add three units to each side of the connection created in the previous step (blue lines).

3 With the thread exiting an edge bead, close the bridge into a tube by adding two Cs, one at a time, and incorporating the second connecting beads from the A and B rings (figure 5, red lines).

Repeat steps 1 through 3 to create a strip of rings and bridges that is two rings wide and eight rings long, alternating rings of A and B.

▶ Embellish

Add embellishments of leaf fringe with drops and chatons or rose montées to the bridges as follows. (Refer to figure 6 for both steps.) Double stitch this work if possible, because it will face the most abrasion.

Leaf Fringe with Drop Pass through a bridge bead (red dot) and string four Ds and two Es; pass back through the first E, string four Ds, and pass through the bridge bead again. Reinforce with a second pass following the same thread path. String one drop, pass through the bridge bead again, reinforce with a second pass, and weave through to exit the next bridge bead shown with a blue dot. Repeat to embellish all bridge beads shown with blue dots.

Montée Add a montée to the middle unit of each bridge as shown.

▶ Finish

Stitch the closed jump rings to the connecting points on the two rings at each end of the bracelet (figure 7). Using chain-nose pliers and open jump rings, connect the lobster claw clasps to one end and the split rings to the other end.

figure 7

RIFF IT

• Embellish with 5-mm rose or chaton montées.

• Make a bracelet that has only one row of rings.

• Explore how different configurations can be made into pendants or earrings.

• Work an odd number of rings into a V-shape and finish with a chain to make a necklace.

• When adding a leaf fringe with drop, vary the number of Cs for shorter or longer leaves.

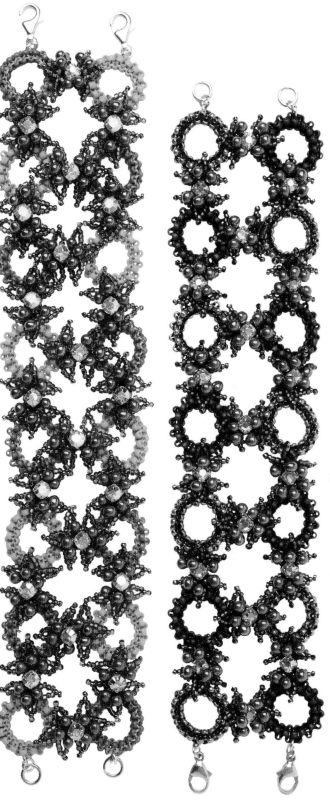

Color variations in Blue in Green (left) and Softly

TWO-BEAT

The bead colors of this project inspired the name—they're reminiscent of the "boom-chick" feel of early jazz, in which the emphasis is on the first and third beat of each measure, rather than on the second and fourth beats of swing. Enjoy a little of your own two-beat.

Made in Stagelight colorway

SUPPLIES

Size 11° silver metallic round seed beads, 4 g

Size 15° gold metallic round seed beads, 4 g

3 inches (7.6 cm) of gold cable link chain, 2 mm

Supplies for beaded toggle, or a purchased clasp

Size 12 beading needles

Golden and gray threads

Sharp snips

Suede or velvet work surface

Wire cutters

TECHNIQUES

Right Angle Weave

4-Drop Bump

Beaded Toggle Closure (optional)

FINISHED SIZE

8½ inches (21.6 cm) long

▶ Overview

Each bead is made entirely of 11° or 15° beads—the process is the same for both sizes. You'll work with a single thread; I used an average-size gray thread with the 11° beads and a thinner gold thread with the 15° beads. Each bead end is stitched to a three-link length of chain, except for the first and last ends, which are stitched to 1-inch (2.5 cm) lengths of chain. You'll add chain to both ends of the first bead. For the second and subsequent beads you'll attach one bead end to the chain from the previous bead and add a new piece to the other end. Make enough beads to reach the desired length.

▶ Base

Create six simple tubes of right angle weave with 11° beads, and five tubes of 15° beads as follows, referring to figure 1 for both steps. **Tip:** For each tube, count out 36 beads. Leave a 6-inch (15.2 cm) thread tail at both ends of the tube to be used later for adding bumps.

1 Weave a four-unit bead base following the red line in figure 1. When closing up the base with the final unit, include one bead from the first unit as shown.

2 Close the units into a ring by passing through 16 beads on both edges of the beadwork and pulling taut (blue line).

▶ Bumps

Using the same bead type as was used for the base, embellish the 16-bead units on both sides of every bead with four rounds of 4-drop bump as follows. **Tip**: Count out 20 beads for each bump.

Bead 1 After cinching the final round of the first bump, add the last link of a 1-inch (2.5 cm) length of chain by stitching through two opposing beads of the final round in a figure-eight pattern (figure 2). **Note:** Adjust the length of this first and the last chain as needed to best fit the toggle bar or other clasp and the overall length of the bracelet. Repeat the thread path until secure. After cinching the final round of the second bump, add the last link of a three-link length of chain.

Bead 2 (Size 15°s) Attach the first bump to the third link of the previous three-link chain, and attach the second bump to the first link of a new three-link chain.

Bead 3 (Size 11°s) Work the same as for bead 2.

Repeat instructions for beads 2 and 3 until you have nine beads linked together, then repeat bead 2 once more.

Final Bead (11°s) Attach the first bump to the third link of the previous three-link chain, and attach the second bump to the first link of a 1-inch (2.5 cm) length of chain.

▶ Finish

If desired, bead a toggle closure. Attach the ending chain lengths to the two parts of the toggle, or to a purchased clasp. (If you make a beaded toggle, work with the same 15°s and stitch the chain ends to the toggle loop and the middle of the toggle bar with the figure-eight method used above.)

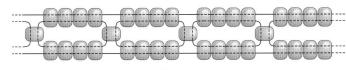

figure 1

figure 2

HIGH STYLE

People in the jazz world have always been conscious of fashion and straight-up looking good. Get your own slice of attention with this little something dangling from your wrist.

Made in Stagelight colorway

SUPPLIES

2-mm round gold-filled beads, approximately 100 per inch (2.5 cm) of finished bracelet*

Size 12 beading needles

Smoke Fireline 6 lb.

Sharp snips

Suede or velvet work surface

* The bracelet shown uses 960 beads. If possible, avoid the small-holed version of 2-mm beads.

TECHNIQUES

Right Angle Weave

3-Drop Bump

Finish with Finial Beads

FINISHED SIZE

Inner circumference, 8 inches (20.3 cm)

▶ Overview

For the base you'll create a simple, closed length of right angle weave, build two sides up from the base, and then bring the sides together to form a fourth side, which will be embellished with bumps. Work with single thread and reinforce when possible for stability. **Note**: Bumps may become lopsided as they're closed. Even out the tension as the final bead is added.

▶ Base Bottom

Leaving a 6-inch (15.2 cm) tail, string 12 beads and tie into a ring with a double knot. Pass through the first three beads strung. String five beads and pass through the last three beads exited and the first four beads just added. Continue in right angle weave to create an alternating series of 12- and eight-bead units until the length fits around a slightly smaller part of the largest part of your hand (the bracelet shown here has 20 large and 19 small units), creating a final small unit that joins the first and last large units (figure 1).

▶ Base Sides

Continue in right angle weave to create alternating eight- and five-bead units on one edge of the bottom piece (figure 2). Repeat on the second edge.

▶ Base Top

Continue in right angle weave to create alternating 12- and 10-bead units that join the sides (figure 3).

▶ Bumps

Embellish the 12-bead units on the top with 3-drop bumps with four rows using 2-mm beads for all rows and cinching the fourth row. Top with a finial bead.

RIFF IT

Don't have the scratch for making one of these babies in a precious metal? Just go with copper or plated beads instead.

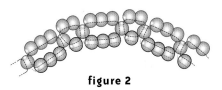

figure 1

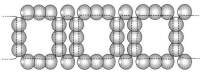

figure 2

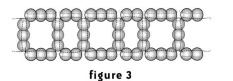

figure 3

107

A view of the interior of the bracelet

SOMETHING COOL

Imagine ducking off the wet sidewalk into a sub-street-level club and finding
June Christy in all her misty, alto-voiced glory. Her body leans into
the piano and she croons "Something Cool" like it's *her* life story.
She would have looked glorious in this cool bracelet.

Made in Nature Girl colorway

▶ Overview

First you'll bezel the rivolis with 15° seed beads in right angle weave and embellish them with ditch beads. Then you'll make a right angle weave base and add risers, which become settings for the rivolis. An extra right angle weave unit becomes a hidden loop clasp.

▶ Rivoli Bezels

Using As, work a strip of 1-drop right angle weave that's 15 units long and two units wide. Bring the short ends of the strip together and join them into a tube by adding a final unit (figure 1).

Work a fast cinch on the front opening, leaving a little slack to be tightened later if needed. Insert a rivoli and work a super-fast cinch on the back opening, again watching the tension. If either opening needs tightening, do that now. Add two rounds of ditch beads to the bezel as follows, referring to figure 2 as you work.

Round 1 With the thread exiting an A of the middle bezel row, string one B and pass through the next A of the same row. Repeat 15 more times. Step up through the first B added (red line).

Round 2 String one C and pass through the next B of the previous row. Repeat 15 more times. Step up through the first C added (blue line).

Set the rivoli aside and repeat nine more times to bezel the remaining stones. *Tip:* If you have thread left after adding ditch beads to the bezel, save it for attaching the bezel to the riser.

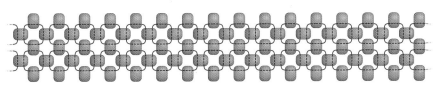

figure 1

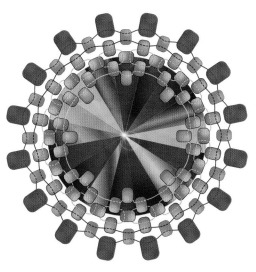

figure 2

SUPPLIES

Size 15° round seed beads:

   A, gray gold matte AB, 5 g

   B, turquoise opaque, < 1 g

Size 11° round seed beads:

   C, bronze metallic matte, 8 g

   D, bronze metallic, 2 g

   E, dusty lavender opaque, < 1 g

10 crystal copper rivolis, 12 mm*

80 gold-lined crystal drop beads, 3.4 mm*

Size 12 beading needles

Gray thread

Sharp snips

Suede or velvet work surface

* To make a shorter bracelet, use 9 rivolis and 72 drop beads; for a longer bracelet, use 11 rivolis and 88 drop beads. A 10-rivoli bracelet snugly fits a 6½-inch (16.5 cm) wrist.

TECHNIQUES

Right Angle Weave Bezel

Ditch Beads

Right Angle Weave

9-Drop Riser

FINISHED SIZE

⅞ x 8 inches (2.2 x 20.3 cm)

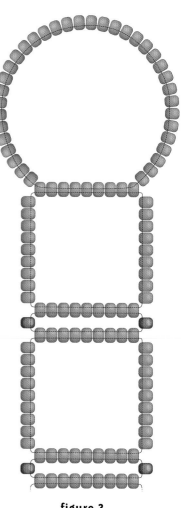

figure 3

▶ Right Angle Weave Base

Following the bead counts in figure 3, work a strip of right angle weave as follows. The first unit will become the clasp loop, and the others will be bases for tubular peyote stitch.

Unit 1 String 45 Cs, tie a simple double knot to form a circle, reinforce, and pass through the first nine Cs strung.

Unit 2 String 27 Cs, then pass through the last nine Cs of the previous unit and through the first 18 Cs just added.

Unit 3 String one D, nine Cs, and one D; pass through the last nine Cs of the previous unit, then through the first D and the first nine Cs just added.

Repeat units 2 and 3 until the base has one loop and ten 36-bead units, ending with a unit 2.

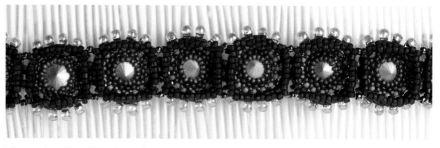

The underside of the bracelet

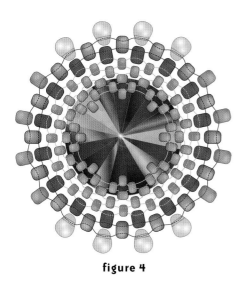

figure 4

▶ Riser

Work three rounds of D into a 9-drop riser on each of the 36-bead base units.

▶ Finish

With the thread still attached to the bezels doubled, or using a new double thread, attach the bezels to the risers and finish the embellishment as follows. If you're working with a single thread, repeat the stitch path for rounds 1 and 2 for added security. Refer to figure 4 for all rounds.

Round 1 Pass through one D in the top round of the riser, then pass through the next C added in round 2 of the bezel. Repeat 15 more times. Pass through the first D again (red line).

Round 2 Add a series of four drops, four Es, four drops, and four Es by passing through Ds of the top riser round used in round 1. Add drops to stick out over the bracelet sides and Es within the creases between components (blue line). ***Note:*** The bead sequence will vary depending on where the needle is exiting the beadwork.

Repeat rounds 1 and 2 to attach and embellish the remaining sections.

Color variations, both in Stagelight

Made in Softly colorway

DOLLED UP

It's Friday night. Throw on your cutest dress, dancing shoes, and a sparkly trinket around your wrist, and you're off in search of the music and adventure woven into the city streets. Cabbies smile, doors open themselves, and you ask yourself, "Wasn't this cocktail more expensive the last time?"

▶ Overview

The large stone and rivolis are bezeled with right angle weave, then they're embellished with extensions of 1-drop bump tubular peyote stitch finished with montées. The components are then connected to each other with more extensions, and finally a beaded toggle or purchased clasp is added with multiple jump rings.

▶ Rivoli Bezel

Working 1-drop right angle weave with a single thread, make five strips of 15° seed beads as outlined below. Do not reinforce the beadwork except to finish old and add new threads.

Base Make one strip four units wide and 35 units long for the stone bezel. Add one more unit to join the strip into a circle. Make four strips three units wide and 23 units long for the rivoli bezels. Add one more unit to join the strips into circles.

Cinch Super-fast cinch the front of the stone bezel, leaving a little slack to be tightened later if needed. Insert the stone and work a super-fast cinch on the back opening, again watching the tension. If either opening needs tightening, do that now. Repeat with a fast cinch on the front and back openings of each rivoli bezel.

▶ Peyote Tube Extensions

Following the instructions on the next page, work extensions of 1-drop tubular peyote stitch up from the bezel surfaces with a single thread and 15°s. Always reinforce the current row before the step up.

Note: In the illustrations, the beads shown with red and pink dots are closest to the stones on the face of the bezel and will have short extensions; the beads shown with dark and light blue dots are in the row below the first set of extensions and will have longer extensions; the beads shown with dark and light green dots are toward the back of the bezel and will have extensions that join the components together.

The underside of the bracelet

SUPPLIES

Size 15° silver metallic round seed beads, 20 g

1 crystal AB stone, 27 mm

4 crystal AB rivolis, 18 mm

82 crystal AB rose montées, 3.5 mm

66 crystal AB chaton montées, 5 mm

4 liquid silver tubes, 5 mm

4 or 6 open silver 20-gauge jump rings, 4 mm

Supplies for beaded toggle, or a purchased clasp

2 square inches (5.1 cm) of garment-weight leather

Leather glue

Size 12 beading needles

Gray thread

Sharp snips

Suede or velvet work surface

Chain-nose pliers

TECHNIQUES

Right Angle Weave Bezel

1-Drop Bump

Montée to 1-Drop Peyote Stitch Tube End

Liquid Silver

Beaded Toggle Closure (optional)

Jump Rings

FINISHED SIZE

7 inches (17.8 cm) long between jump rings

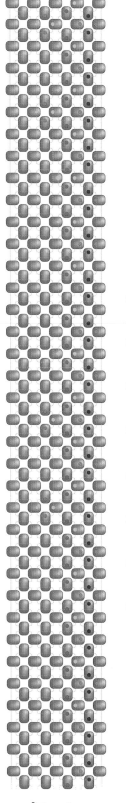

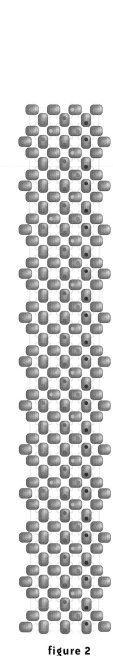

figure 1   **figure 2**

Large Stone Embellishment

Refer to figure 1 for all extensions. Each unit consists of a set of four beads: two red and two pink, or two dark blue and two light blue, or two dark green and two light green.

Short Extensions Weave through the beadwork to exit a bead illustrated with a red dot. String one bead and pass through the other bead in the same unit illustrated with a red dot; string one bead and pass through the first bead exited. Repeat the thread path and step up through the first bead added. **Note:** The beads added in this round will sit atop the base beads illustrated with pink dots. *String one bead and pass through the next bead added in the previous round, then string one bead and pass through the next bead added in the previous round. Repeat the thread path and step up through the first bead added in the round. Repeat from * to work six rounds total and finish with a rose montée. Work a short extension from each unit illustrated with red and pink dots, for 18 total.

Long Extensions Weave through the beadwork to exit a bead illustrated with a dark blue dot. String one bead and pass through the other bead in the same unit illustrated with a dark blue dot; string one bead and pass through the first bead exited. Repeat the thread path and step up through the first beaded added. **Note:** The beads added in this round will sit atop the base beads illustrated with light blue dots. *String one bead, pass through the next bead added in the previous round, string one bead, and pass through the next bead added in the previous round. Repeat the thread path and step up through the first bead added in the round. Repeat from * to work eight rounds total and finish with a chaton montée. Work a long extension from each unit illustrated with blue dots, for 18 total.

Connecting Extensions Weave through the beadwork to exit a bead illustrated with a dark green dot. String one bead and pass through the other bead in the same unit illustrated with a dark green dot; string one bead, and pass through the first bead exited. Repeat the thread path and step up through the first bead added. **Note:** The beads added in this round will sit atop the base beads illustrated with light green dots. *String one bead and pass through the next bead

added in the previous round, then string one bead and pass through the next bead added in the previous round. Repeat the thread path and step up through the first bead added in the round. Repeat from * to work 20 rounds total. Work a connecting extension from each unit illustrated with green dots, for four total.

Rivoli Embellishment

Refer to figure 2 for all extensions. Each unit consists of a set of four beads: either two red and two pink, or two dark blue and two light blue, or two dark green and two light green.

Short Extensions Work as for the short extensions on the large stone, except that each extension has four rounds instead of six. Each rivoli has 12 short extensions.

Long Extensions Work as for the long extensions on the large stone, except that each extension has four rounds instead of eight. Each rivoli has 12 long extensions.

Connecting Extensions On two of the rivolis, work as for the connecting extensions on the large stone, but work 20-round extensions over only two adjacent units illustrated with green dots. On the other two rivolis, work 25-round extensions over one unit illustrated with green dots and connect the last row to the adjacent unit illustrated with green dots. At the midway point of the resulting loops, stitch in one seed bead, one liquid silver tube, and one seed bead to form small loops for connecting the toggle clasp. Repeat the thread path to reinforce.

▶ Finish

With the large component at the center flanked by the small components without loops, stitch the extensions from the large component to the extensionless sides of the small components through the beads illustrated with light green dots. Stitch the extensions from the attached small components to the extensionless side of the components with loops through the beads illustrated with light green dots.

Make a beaded toggle embellished with rose montées. Instead of stitching in a closed jump ring at the center of the loop and the toggle, make a loop of one seed bead, one liquid silver tube, and one more seed bead. Using double or triple jump ring connections, connect the clasp ends to the corresponding loops on the end components.

RIFF IT

• Stitch fewer rounds in the connecting extensions for a shorter bracelet; the extensions with montées will overlap when lying flat and will curve nicely when on the wrist.

• Make a lovely and eye-catching pendant with just one component.

• Finish with 3-mm crystals instead of montées.

• Stitch a pin back to one component and wear it as a brooch.

Color variations in Nature Girl (left) and in orange

GALLERY

I asked some notable beadwork artists—as well as some whose work you may not have seen before—for their best pieces featuring combinations of right angle weave and peyote. Just as fine musicians improvise over the 32-bar changes and bare their souls, these bead artists reveal their pith in the challenge of combining stitches.

LEFT

ELIZABETH PENN

Leahy Street Earrings #1, 2009

8.3 x 1.5 cm

Seed beads, sterling silver, nylon; right angle weave, peyote stitch, wirework

PHOTO BY RACHEL NELSON-SMITH

BOTTOM

AMY KATZ

Ooh La Links, 2009

2.5 x 19.1 cm

Seed beads, glass pearls, crystals

PHOTO BY CARRIE JOHNSON

TOP

MET INNMON

Roxanne's Fan, 2010

34 x 8 x 0.7 cm

Seed beads; tubular right angle weave, flat right angle weave, odd-count peyote stitch, picot edging

PHOTO BY LARRY HANSEN

RIGHT

LOUISE HILL

Cupola House, 2010

13 x 11.5 x 11.5 cm

Resin, no-fire clay, bicones, seed beads, hot-fix crystals, crystal, nailhead beads; three-dimensional and flat right angle weave

PHOTO BY ARTIST

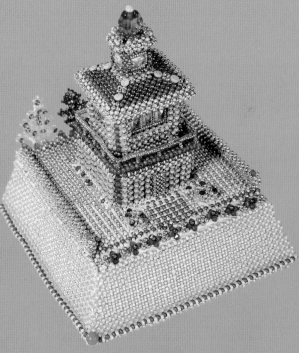

LEFT

NANC MEINHARDT

Rose Bracelet, 2010

3.8 x 16.2 x 5.1 cm

Seed beads, vintage sequins, vintage silk flowers, nylon thread, metal closure; 2-drop peyote stitch, 3-drop peyote stitch, right angle weave, embellishment, picot

PHOTO BY MARTIN KONOPACKI

**MARCIA DECOSTER
HEATHER TRIMLETT
DALLAS BEAD SOCIETY**

Untitled, 2010

53 x 25 x 3 cm

Seed beads, crystals; right angle
weave, peyote stitch

PHOTO BY ARTIST

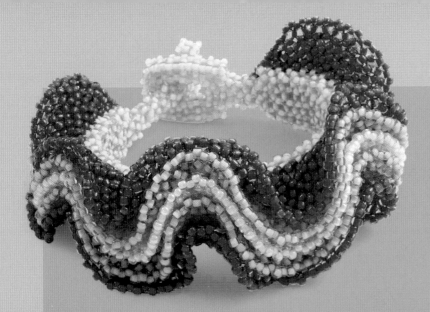

TOP

TERI DANNENBERG

The Wave, 2009

20.3 x 3.8 x 1.3 cm

Seed beads; three-dimensional
right angle weave, peyote stitch

PHOTO BY EMILY B. MILLER

LEFT

ELIZABETH PENN

Leahy Street Earrings #2, 2009

7.6 x 1 cm

Seed beads, sterling silver, nylon; right angle
weave, peyote stitch, wirework

PHOTO BY RACHEL NELSON-SMITH

RIGHT

JEANNETTE COOK

All Buckled Up Cuff, 2008

40 x 17 cm

Delica beads, bicones; right
angle weave, peyote stitch

PHOTO BY RACHEL NELSON-SMITH

LEFT

SUSAN KAZARIAN

Home Sweet Home, 2010

5 x 2.5 x 3 cm

Seed beads; right angle weave, even-count peyote stitch, herringbone weave

PHOTO BY RACHEL NELSON-SMITH

BOTTOM

PAMM HORBIT

Nitidus Quasar, 2010

12.5 x 12.5 x 12.5 cm

Cylinder beads, pearls, amethysts, rivolis; odd- and even-count peyote stitch, right angle weave

PHOTO BY SARA TRO

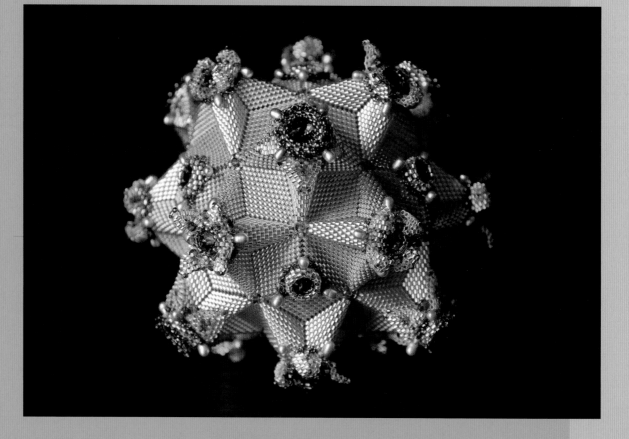

CAROL CYPHER

Triad of Jade Triangles Necklace, 2010

20.5 x 18 x 0.5 cm

Seed beads, magnetic closure; right angle weave, peyote stitch

PHOTO BY ARTIST

MARCIA DECOSTER

Aberge, 2009

18 x 5 x 1 cm

Seed beads, crystals; right angle weave, peyote stitch

PHOTO BY ARTIST

121

RIGHT

SUZANNE GOLDEN

Orange/Purple Bracelet, 2009

2.8 x 7 cm

Seed beads, crystal bicones; right angle weave, angle stitch, embellished

PHOTO BY ROBERT DIAMANTE

LEFT

JEANNETTE COOK

May's Garden Necklace, 2007

30 x 18 x 5 cm

Leaves, flowers, seed beads, drop beads, red coral

PHOTO BY RACHEL NELSON-SMITH

LEFT

Confluence, **2009**

38.1 x 20.3 x 2.5 cm

Glass, lampwork by Patty Lakinsmith, nylon, sterling silver; right angle weave, netting, wirework

PHOTO BY ARTIST

BOTTOM

Life's a Circus Cuff, **2009**

7.6 x 10.2 x 5.1 cm

Glass, crystal, brass, velvet, nylon; bead embroidery, peyote stitch, fringe

123

TOP

O. Bersten Specimen, 2009

50.8 x 38.1 x 2.5 cm

Glass, crystals, nylon, gold; right angle weave, peyote stitch

PHOTO BY ARTIST

MIDDLE

Sea Star Bangles, 2008

Grouping, 15.2 x 15.2 x 15.2 cm

Glass, nylon; peyote stitch, right angle weave

PHOTO BY ARTIST

BOTTOM

Beon Freo Cuff, 2008

3.8 x 17.8 x 8.9 cm

Glass, crystal, acrylic, nylon, sterling silver; wirework, peyote stitch, herringbone, square stitch, herringbone/square stitch, right angle weave, fringe

LEFT

Tongues and Torsos, 2009

45.7 x 20.3 x 3.8 cm

Glass, lampwork by Ronit Dagan, silk, nylon, gold; peyote stitch, netting, fringe

PHOTO BY ARTIST

RIGHT

Torso, 2010

7.6 x 3.8 cm

Glass, nylon, gold chain; brick stitch

LEFT

Frog Ring, **2009**

1.9 x 1.9 x 3.2 cm

Lampwork by Wayne Robbins, glass, nylon; peyote stitch, fringe

RIGHT

Ootheca Cuff Sterling, **2010**

6.4 x 10.2 x 10.2 cm

Sterling silver, crystals, polypropylene; right angle weave, peyote stitch, wirework

ABOUT THE AUTHOR

Rachel Nelson-Smith is a master beadweaver whose work is a blend of fabrication techniques. With a sense of adventure, her imagination shapes bold and dynamic pieces. She uses color and its energy extensively to create work that reflects the world she sees around her.

This is Rachel's second book. Examples of her vibrant work have appeared in numerous publications. Her seven projects in Kate Shoup Welsh's *Not Your Mama's Beading* established her virtuosity. In *Masters: Beadweaving*, she was featured with other contemporary beadweaving masters. Rachel's contributions to instructional jewelry-making books by Sharilyn Miller and in *Marcia DeCoster's Beaded Opulence* and *500 Silver Jewelry Designs* demonstrate her ability to capture the muse.

Rachel pushes the boundaries of improvisational beadweaving. Since 1996, she has taught basic to advanced classes in the California Bay Area; she's led workshops for the South Bay Bead Art Guild, the South Florida Jewelry Arts Guild, the Bead Society of Northern Virginia, the Wild West Bead Society of Fort Worth-Texas, and the Bead Society of Greater New York, to name just a few; and she's been an instructor in bead stores across the United States, internationally, and privately.

PHOTO BY JEFFREY JAY LUHN

Since 2005, her designs have been available at national bead shows, including the Bead&Button Show and Puget Sound Bead Festival, and around the United States in bead stores and for bead societies. Rachel also schedules speaking engagements in various parts of the country.

Visit her website, www.rachelnelsonsmith.com, where you'll find additional photos of her beadwork, teaching schedule, and more.

ACKNOWLEDGMENTS

To the two people beside me through thicket and thin wood—Maud Pruiett, whose child I'll always be; and Colin Smith, I know not where I'd be without you. Thank you for your love and support.

For skillfully framing my work, thank you to Nathalie Mornu and all the Lark Jewelry & Beading staff who worked on this book. Thank you to technical editor Judith Durant for making sense of the words and numbers, and to art director Carol Barnao and photographer Lynne Harty for making the images and pages sing. To Ray Hemachandra and Lark, I am humbled that you've included my work in your distinctly excellent Beadweaving Master Class series.

Volumes of thanks go to Liz Penn for all the hours spent diligently beading the variations with dedication and care.

To Winny Stockwell, Susan Kazarian, Marcia DeCoster, Mary VerVoort, Jenny Leech, JoJo McLeod, and Margaret Loos, I'm grateful for your guidance and inspiration. When one fails to believe, it's helpful to have friends and teachers like these. Ron Rock, thank you for keeping me hip to the color trends.

A special thanks to Michael Parker for asking if I'd be interested in jazz and for bringing this remarkable art form into view. Kris Stephens, Nick Beason, Roger Letson, James Durland, Steve Newman, Nate Pruitt, and Chuy Varela were the beacons of my jazz education and I'm grateful for their influence in my life.

Grateful acknowledgments go to the band members pictured in this book: Benny Torres on saxophone, Kent Cressman on piano, Drew Plant on bass, and Steve Robertson on drums. Thanks for playing with me that night and for agreeing to appear in these pages. Thanks, too, to Walter Wagner for coming out to photograph us, and to Pete Escovedo for the gig.

A final maxim from one of my favorite tunes to sing, eden ahbez's "Nature Boy":

"The greatest thing you'll ever learn, is just to love and be loved in return."

INDEX

AN ESSENTIAL LIBRARY OF BOOKS FOR BEADERS

Diane Fitzgerald's **SHAPED BEADWORK** — dimensional jewelry with peyote stitch

Diane Fitzgerald

Marcia DeCoster's **BEADED OPULENCE** — elegant jewelry projects with right angle weave

Marcia DeCoster

Laura McCabe's **EMBELLISHED BEADWEAVING** — jewelry lavished with fringe, fronds, lacework & more

Laura McCabe

Sherry Serafini's **SENSATIONAL BEAD EMBROIDERY** — 25 inspiring jewelry projects

Sherry Serafini

MAGGIE MEISTER'S **CLASSICAL ELEGANCE** — 20 beaded jewelry designs

Maggie Meister

RACHEL NELSON-SMITH'S **BEAD RIFFS** — Jewelry Projects in Peyote & Right Angle Weave

Rachel Nelson-Smith